The Book On

Re-Unifying Society

The Book On Series
Jordan L. Monroe

Published by The Book On Publishing, 2025.
First edition. October 19, 2025.

Website: https://thebookon.ca
Substack: https://thebookonpublishing.substack.com/

The Book On Re-Unifying Society
First edition. October 19, 2025.

Copyright © 2025 The Book On Publishing
ISBN: 978-1-997909-38-5

Written by Jordan L. Monroe

The Book On Series

Table Of Contents

Chapter 1: The Fractured Tapestry

The fabric of our shared existence has become a paradox of our times. We live in an era of unprecedented connectivity, where a device in our pocket can instantly reach billions of people worldwide. Yet, we have never felt more isolated from one another. The grand tapestry that once depicted a society bound by common threads of understanding, shared values, and mutual recognition has been pulled apart at its seams, leaving us with fragments that barely acknowledge their connection to the whole. This fragmentation is not merely a political phenomenon, though politics amplifies it considerably, nor is it simply a cultural divide, though culture shapes its expression. Instead, it represents a fundamental rupture in the social contract that binds human beings together in collective enterprise. We have witnessed the dissolution of the commons—those shared spaces, both physical and conceptual, where citizens once gathered to negotiate difference and forge consensus. Town squares have emptied as digital echo chambers have filled. Community institutions that once served as meeting grounds for diverse perspectives have weakened or disappeared entirely. Religious congregations, civic organizations, labor unions, and neighborhood associations— the traditional intermediary institutions that Alexis de Tocqueville identified as essential to democratic life—have seen their membership and influence decline precipitously. In their absence, we have lost not just venues for interaction, but the very habits of engagement that made coexistence possible among people who disagreed. The result is a society increasingly characterized by mutual incomprehension, where different segments of the population not only hold different views but inhabit entirely different informational

1

universes, subscribe to incompatible narratives about basic facts, and view one another not as fellow citizens with whom they disagree but as existential threats to be defeated rather than neighbors to be understood.

The origins of this fracture are multiple and overlapping, defying simple explanation or singular causation. Economic transformations over the past half-century have fundamentally reordered the landscape of opportunity and security that once underpinned social cohesion. The post-World War II consensus that generated broadly shared prosperity in many developed nations—the era when a single income could support a family, when pensions were reliable, when each generation expected to live better than the last—has given way to an economy characterized by precarity, inequality, and winner-take-all dynamics. Manufacturing jobs that once anchored working-class communities have disappeared, outsourced to distant nations, or replaced by automation, leaving behind economic devastation and social disintegration. The communities most affected have experienced not merely financial hardship but a comprehensive unraveling of the social fabric: rising rates of substance abuse, family dissolution, declining life expectancy, and a pervasive sense of abandonment by institutions and elites who once promised to represent their interests. Meanwhile, metropolitan centers have surged ahead, concentrating wealth, education, and opportunity in ways that have created not just economic inequality but also geographical segregation of life experiences. Those who have thrived in the knowledge economy increasingly live in different neighborhoods, attend other schools, work in various industries, and consume different media than those left behind by economic restructuring. This geographic and economic sorting has profound implications for social unity, as it means that people across different economic strata rarely encounter one another in the ordinary course of life, breeding unfamiliarity and eroding the sense of shared fate that undergirds social solidarity.

Technological disruption has accelerated these fractures while introducing entirely new dimensions of social fragmentation. The information revolution promised to democratize knowledge and bring humanity together, yet it has enabled the creation of parallel realities that share ever less common ground. Social media platforms, engineered to maximize engagement through algorithms that prioritize emotional arousal, have created incentive structures that reward the most divisive, inflammatory, and extreme content. These platforms have democratized voice in unprecedented ways, allowing marginalized perspectives to find audiences and enabling horizontal communication that bypasses traditional gatekeepers. However, this democratization has come with profound costs to our collective capacity for sense-making and truth-determination. The same technologies that connect us also sort us into increasingly homogeneous networks where our existing beliefs are constantly reinforced and dissenting views rarely penetrate. We curate our information feeds to exclude discomfort, surrounding ourselves with content that confirms what we already believe. The concept of shared reality—the baseline agreement about observable facts that must exist for productive disagreement about values and policies—has eroded as different communities literally see other events, or the same events filtered through divergent interpretive frameworks, that they might as well be different. The January 6th Capitol riot, the COVID-19 pandemic, climate change, and police violence—these and countless other events are processed through radically different epistemic frameworks that leave citizens with incompatible understandings not just of what these events mean but of what actually happened. This represents a crisis not merely of disagreement but of the very possibility of shared perception that must precede any negotiation of difference.

The transformation of media from a centralized, gate-kept system to a fragmented, democratized ecosystem has played a central role in this epistemic crisis. For most of the twentieth century, despite its flaws and biases, the broadcast media model created shared informational touchstones. Millions of Americans watched the same evening news programs, read the same major newspapers, and thus operated from a baseline of common information, even when they disagreed about interpretation and policy implications. This system had significant limitations—it often excluded marginalized voices, reinforced elite perspectives, and could be misleading or propagandistic. Yet it did create a common informational foundation that made dialogue possible across differences. The internet shattered this model, replacing it with infinite choice and algorithmic curation. We now inhabit a media landscape where individuals can construct entirely customized informational diets that never challenge their preexisting worldviews. Conservative Americans can consume a steady stream of content from sources that validate conservative perspectives while portraying liberals as threats to civilization. Progressive Americans can immerse themselves in media ecosystems that depict conservatives as bigoted authoritarians. Neither side presents the other's best arguments; only caricatures designed to provoke outrage. The business model of digital media—dependent on attention capture and advertising revenue—creates relentless pressure toward sensationalism, simplification, and emotional manipulation. Nuance, complexity, and ambiguity—the essential ingredients of mature democratic discourse—are algorithmically disadvantaged because they do not generate the engagement metrics that platforms prioritize. The result is a public sphere that privileges heat over light, outrage over understanding, and tribal solidarity over truth-seeking.

Cultural and demographic changes have introduced additional fault lines that strain the bonds of collective identity. Societies across the developed world are experiencing rapid diversification along multiple dimensions—race, ethnicity, religion, language, and cultural practice. This diversification represents, in many respects, a fulfillment of liberal democratic ideals of equality and inclusion, as previously marginalized groups claim their rightful place in the civic and cultural mainstream. Immigration has enriched receiving societies with new perspectives, skills, and cultural traditions. Social movements have successfully challenged hierarchies and exclusions that once seemed natural and inevitable. Women have entered the workforce and leadership positions in unprecedented numbers. LGBTQ individuals have claimed public recognition and legal rights. These transformations represent genuine moral progress, expansions of the circle of dignity and citizenship. However, rapid demographic and cultural change also generates anxiety, particularly among populations who perceive themselves as losing status or cultural dominance. The reaction against multiculturalism and demographic change has fueled populist movements across the Western world, from Brexit to the election of Donald Trump to the rise of right-wing parties in Europe. These movements tap into genuine fears about cultural displacement, economic insecurity, and loss of community, even as they sometimes channel these anxieties toward scapegoating and exclusion. The challenge for societies committed to both diversity and unity is navigating how to welcome and include new members while maintaining sufficient cultural coherence to sustain collective action and mutual obligation. This requires more than mere tolerance; it demands the construction of overarching identities and narratives capacious enough to encompass difference while providing a foundation for solidarity.

The weakening of shared institutions and rituals has left us without the regular practices of coming together that once reinforced social bonds across lines of difference. Consider the transformation of public space in American life.

Town halls, public parks, libraries, and main streets—these once served as commons where citizens of different backgrounds encountered one another, negotiated shared norms, and developed the familiarity that breeds civic friendship. Many of these spaces have declined or disappeared, replaced by privatized alternatives that facilitate economic transactions but not social connections. We shop at big-box stores or online rather than neighborhood businesses where we know the proprietor. We watch streaming services in isolation rather than gathering in movie theaters. We exercise in home gyms or boutique studios, segregated by price point rather than public recreation centers. We attend schools that are increasingly segregated by race and class as residential patterns sort us into homogeneous neighborhoods, and school choice programs allow families to opt out of common institutions. Even religious participation, once a powerful force for community building, has declined dramatically, with the fastest-growing religious category being the "nones"—those with no religious affiliation. The military draft, which once mixed Americans across class and regional lines in standard national service, ended generations ago. All of these changes have cumulatively reduced the touchpoints where Americans of different backgrounds, beliefs, and life circumstances encounter one another as fellow citizens rather than as abstractions or stereotypes. Without regular interaction, without the friction and accommodation that come from sharing space and negotiating difference, we lose the skills and habits essential to democratic coexistence.

Political polarization both reflects and accelerates these underlying fractures, creating a self-reinforcing cycle of mutual antagonism and institutional dysfunction. The American political system has sorted into two increasingly homogeneous parties that align along multiple dimensions simultaneously—not just ideology but also geography, race, religion, education, and cultural values. This "big sort" means that political identity has become a master identity that correlates with and reinforces countless other aspects of life. Democrats and Republicans not only vote differently but live in different places, attend different churches (or none at all), consume different media, and even prefer other brands and leisure activities. Political scientists have documented increasing "affective polarization"—dislike and distrust of the opposing party—that now exceeds racial and religious prejudice in some measurements. Many Americans report that they would be upset if their child married someone from the opposing political party, a sentiment that would have seemed absurd a generation ago. This polarization infects our institutions, making governance increasingly difficult as compromise becomes politically untenable and obstruction becomes the default strategy. Legislative bodies that once operated on the assumption that members would disagree on policy while sharing commitment to the institution and the nation have become arenas of all-out warfare where the goal is not legislative accomplishment but theatrical performance for tribal audiences. The nomination of judges, once a relatively nonpartisan affair, has become one of the most intensely contested flashpoints of political combat. Even scientific and public health institutions have become polarized, as responses to COVID-19 demonstrated, with basic protective measures like masking becoming symbols of political identity rather than pragmatic public health responses.

The economic consequences of this fracture are profound and often underappreciated. Market economies depend on trust—trust that contracts will be honored, that institutions will enforce rules fairly, and that strangers can engage in mutually beneficial exchange. Social capital — the network of relationships and norms that facilitate cooperation — has been identified by economists as crucial to prosperity. When societies fragment and trust declines, economic efficiency suffers. Transactions become more costly as parties must invest in protection against fraud and defection. Corruption increases as universal norms give way to particularistic loyalties. Innovation slows because entrepreneurship requires cooperation across networks that span different communities. Infrastructure investment becomes difficult because citizens cannot agree on collective priorities or trust that resources will be used fairly. The failure to address climate change, despite overwhelming scientific consensus about the threat, exemplifies how social fracture undermines our capacity for collective action on shared challenges. Climate change represents a problem that requires coordination across nations, generations, and ideological divides. Yet, our fractured societies struggle to mount effective responses because we cannot agree on basic facts, cannot trust institutions to implement solutions fairly, and cannot subordinate immediate tribal interests to long-term collective welfare. The same dynamic plays out in countless policy domains—healthcare, education, criminal justice, immigration—where our inability to forge consensus or even engage in good-faith negotiation means that problems fester while solutions remain out of reach.

The psychological and emotional toll of living in a fractured society is enormous, though often invisible in conventional metrics. Human beings are intensely social creatures, evolved for life in small groups where cooperation and mutual recognition were essential to survival. We possess powerful drives toward belonging and tribal solidarity, as well as capacities for empathy, perspective-taking, and collaboration with strangers that enabled our ancestors to build large-scale societies. The current environment activates our tribal instincts while frustrating our capacities for broader identification and cooperation. Many people report feeling exhausted by constant political conflict, anxious about the future, and alienated from neighbors and even family members with whom they disagree politically. The sense that we are locked in existential conflict with our fellow citizens, that the other side represents not merely mistaken beliefs but fundamental threats to everything we value, generates chronic stress and diminishes well-being. Studies have documented increasing rates of depression, anxiety, and loneliness, particularly among younger generations who have come of age during this period of intensifying social fragmentation. The suicide rate has increased significantly over the past two decades. Drug overdose deaths have skyrocketed, particularly in communities hit hardest by economic dislocation. These are not merely individual tragedies but social phenomena, symptoms of broken social bonds and collapsed collective meaning. The philosopher Charles Taylor has written about the importance of "social imaginaries"—the shared understandings of how we fit together in common enterprise. When these imaginaries fracture, when we can no longer perceive ourselves as members of a common project, the psychological consequences are severe.

The challenge of re-unifying a fractured society is complicated by the fact that not all fractures are problematic, and not all unity is desirable. History provides abundant examples of enforced unity that suppressed difference through oppression and exclusion. The social cohesion of 1950s America, often invoked nostalgically, rested in part on the subordination of women, the segregation of African Americans, the closeting of LGBTQ individuals, and the cultural marginalization of religious and ethnic minorities. Any project of social re-unification must grapple with the reality that previous forms of unity were often purchased through injustice, and that the fracturing we now experience is partly the result of previously excluded groups claiming voice and demanding inclusion. The task is not to return to a mythical past of harmonious consensus, but to forge new forms of unity compatible with pluralism, capable of encompassing profound difference while maintaining the social cohesion necessary for collective action and mutual obligation. This requires distinguishing between fractures that reflect healthy pluralism and those that undermine the conditions for coexistence. A society where citizens hold different religious beliefs, practice different cultural traditions, and pursue other life paths exhibits pluralism, not fracture. A society where citizens cannot agree on basic facts, view one another as enemies, and lack shared institutions or practices that bring them together exhibits fractures that threaten the viability of collective self-governance.

Throughout human history, societies have developed various mechanisms for managing differences while maintaining cohesion. Kinship systems, religious traditions, shared enemies, charismatic leaders, powerful myths and narratives—all have served to bind people together despite their differences. Modern liberal democracies face a particular challenge: they aspire to unity without coercion, to collective action without authoritarianism, and to shared identity without ethnic or religious exclusion. Liberal democracy promises that people of profound difference can nonetheless recognize one another as fellow citizens with equal dignity, can deliberate together about collective concerns, and can accept outcomes even when they lose because they trust the process and their fellow citizens. This promise has always been fragile and imperfectly realized, but it has proven remarkably successful in creating stable, prosperous, and free societies. The current fracture crisis represents a test of whether this model can survive in an age of technological disruption, economic transformation, and rapid cultural change. The answer will depend on whether we can develop new institutions, practices, and narratives that perform the unifying functions that older mechanisms once served. This will require creativity, experimentation, and a willingness to learn from both historical wisdom and contemporary innovation.

The path forward requires acknowledging complexity and resisting simplistic solutions. There is no single villain responsible for our fractured condition, and thus no single hero who can save us. The fragmentation we experience emerges from the interaction of economic, technological, cultural, and political forces, each influencing the others in complex feedback loops. Addressing this challenge will require operating on multiple levels simultaneously—reforming institutions, developing new practices, changing cultural narratives, and cultivating individual capacities for perspective-taking and dialogue across difference. It will require both structural changes to reduce inequality and create genuine opportunity, and cultural changes to rebuild the norms and habits that make coexistence possible. It will require both preserving hard-won gains in inclusion and recognition and developing overarching identities and commitments that bind us together despite our differences. The project of re-unifying society is not about eliminating difference or enforcing conformity, but about rebuilding the social infrastructure—both material and cultural—that makes it possible for different people to recognize their mutual dependence, negotiate their disagreements, and cooperate in pursuit of shared flourishing. The stakes could hardly be higher. A society that cannot maintain minimal cohesion cannot address its collective challenges, cannot provide security and opportunity for its members, and cannot preserve the freedoms that make individual flourishing possible. The fracturing we now experience, if left unaddressed, threatens not merely our prosperity but our capacity for self-governance and our viability as a political community.

The chapters that follow will explore how we might undertake this work of reunification, examining both the obstacles we face and the resources available to overcome them. We will investigate how to rebuild shared institutions and create new spaces for encounter across difference. We will consider how to reform our information ecosystem to make truth-seeking and mutual understanding more possible. We will explore how to address the economic foundations of fracture through policies that create genuine opportunity and shared prosperity. We will examine how to cultivate the individual and collective capacities—empathy, humility, perspective-taking, and dialogue skills—that are essential to democratic coexistence. We will draw on examples from communities and movements that have successfully bridged divides, learning from their successes and failures. The task is daunting — perhaps unprecedented in its complexity — but not impossible. Human beings have repeatedly demonstrated the capacity to expand the circle of recognition, to build communities across difference, and to create institutions that enable cooperation among strangers. The fractured tapestry can be rewoven —not into a uniform cloth but into a richer, more inclusive fabric that preserves its varied threads while binding them together in a common purpose. This is the work before us, and the future of our shared life together depends on our willingness to undertake it.

The question of how fractured societies have historically moved toward greater cohesion offers both cautionary tales and sources of hope. The post-Civil War reconciliation in America, though deeply flawed in its abandonment of Reconstruction's promises to formerly enslaved people, demonstrated that even societies torn by armed conflict can eventually forge working arrangements. Germany's post-World War II transformation from totalitarian aggressor to democratic peace-builder required not just institutional reform but a profound cultural reckoning with historical atrocity. South Africa's transition from apartheid, while still grappling with enormous inequalities and unresolved tensions, showed how truth-telling and symbolic acts of recognition could create space for former enemies to begin coexisting as citizens. These examples remind us that social repair is possible even after profound rupture. Still, they also illustrate that such repair is neither quick nor complete, requiring sustained commitment across generations and often leaving unhealed wounds that continue to shape collective life.

What distinguishes our current moment from these historical precedents is the simultaneous combination of technological acceleration, economic anxiety, and cultural transformation. Previous periods of social stress typically involved one or two major disruptions—industrialization accompanied by labor strife, or demographic change accompanied by nativist backlash, or economic depression accompanied by political extremism. Our era compounds multiple transformations: the internet revolution fundamentally altering how we communicate and process information; globalization and automation reshaping employment and community stability; demographic shifts changing the composition of populations; climate change threatening basic systems of life support; and now, increasingly, artificial intelligence promising to disrupt knowledge work in ways that could make previous economic dislocations seem modest by comparison. This accumulation of simultaneous disruptions strains our adaptive capacities, overwhelming the slower processes of cultural adjustment and institutional evolution that have historically helped societies navigate change.

Moreover, the scale of contemporary challenges extends beyond what any single nation can address independently. Yet, our fractured condition makes even national-level cooperation difficult, let alone the international coordination required to address transnational threats. Climate change, pandemic disease, nuclear proliferation, financial contagion, migration flows, terrorism—these challenges respect no borders and require coordinated responses across societies that are themselves internally divided. The irony is bitter: precisely when we need unprecedented levels of cooperation, both within and between nations, our capacity for collective action has atrophied. The institutions built after World War II to facilitate international collaboration—the United Nations, the World Bank, the International Monetary Fund, various treaty organizations—face legitimacy crises and seem inadequate to contemporary challenges. New forms of global governance struggle to emerge because nations jealously guard sovereignty and domestic populations distrust distant bureaucracies. Meanwhile, the problems requiring collective response continue to intensify, indifferent to our political divisions and institutional inadequacies.

The role of leadership in either exacerbating or ameliorating social fracture deserves particular attention. Political leaders face powerful incentives to exploit division rather than bridge it, as polarization energizes base voters and simplifies fundraising. The most successful politicians in recent years have often been those who most effectively channeled grievance and antagonism, who positioned themselves as warriors for their tribe against enemy tribes, who offered simple narratives of good versus evil rather than acknowledging complexity and trade-offs. This is not historically unusual—demagogues have consistently recognized the political potency of activating tribal instincts and identifying scapegoats. What has changed is the media environment that amplifies and rewards such strategies, and the weakening of party institutions and intermediary organizations that once constrained the most divisive impulses. Reversing this dynamic requires not just individual leaders of unusual courage and vision, but also structural reforms that change the incentives facing political actors. Electoral systems that punish extremism and reward coalition-building, campaign finance reforms that reduce dependence on the most ideologically intense donors, media regulations that limit the most egregious forms of manipulation and misinformation—these institutional changes could create environments where bridging leaders have better chances of success than dividing demagogues.

Chapter 2: Echoes of Division

The divisions that fragment contemporary society do not arise spontaneously from a vacuum, nor do they represent entirely novel phenomena in human history. Instead, they are echoes—reverberations of ancient tribal patterns, historic grievances, and cyclical fears that resonate through time with increasing amplitude. These echoes bounce off the walls of our institutions, distort as they pass through our media ecosystems, and return to us transformed yet hauntingly familiar. Understanding how past divisions echo into the present requires examining not just the origins of our current rifts, but the mechanisms by which historical patterns of separation perpetuate themselves across generations, adapting to new contexts while maintaining their fundamental character. The psychological, cultural, and structural reverberations of past divisions shape our present landscape in ways we often fail to recognize, creating feedback loops that amplify discord and make reconciliation increasingly difficult. By tracing these echoes back to their sources and understanding how they propagate, we can begin to identify points of intervention where the cycle might be disrupted and the amplitude of division gradually diminished.

Consider how the geographic divisions of the American Civil War continue to structure political behavior more than a century and a half after the conflict's conclusion. Counties that voted for secession in 1861 show statistically significant correlations with voting patterns in contemporary elections, even when controlling for current economic conditions, demographic composition, and educational levels. This is not because the specific issues of slavery and states' rights remain active political questions in their original form, but because the social identities forged in that crucible of conflict have been transmitted across generations through family stories, local institutions, regional pride, and collective memory. The grandchildren and great-grandchildren of Confederate soldiers may hold vastly different explicit beliefs about race and federal authority than their ancestors. Yet, their political affiliations and attitudes toward centralized power often reflect the same underlying disposition toward autonomy and suspicion of external control that animated their forebears. Similarly, communities in the industrial North that sent regiments to fight for the Union maintain distinct political cultures that emphasize national unity and social progress, even as the economic conditions that once defined these regions have transformed beyond recognition. These geographic echoes demonstrate how spatial patterns of division can outlive the original conflicts that created them, becoming embedded in regional identities that persist across dramatic social and economic changes.

The echoes of religious conflicts present another compelling illustration of how historical divisions reverberate into contemporary discord. The Protestant-Catholic tensions that convulsed Europe for centuries and sparked wars that killed millions have not vanished but rather transformed and migrated into new contexts. In Northern Ireland, the Troubles that dominated the latter half of the twentieth century drew their intensity not merely from contemporary disputes over governance and national identity, but from centuries of accumulated grievance, massacre, dispossession, and mutual antagonism dating back to the Plantation of Ulster in the 1600s. Each generation inherited stories of victimization and resistance, each community maintained its own martyrology of heroes and tragedies, and each side viewed the other through a lens ground by hundreds of years of conflict. The specific theological disputes between Protestantism and Catholicism that once motivated these divisions have receded in importance for most participants—Northern Ireland today is increasingly secular, and many young people struggle to articulate the doctrinal differences between the traditions that supposedly divide them. Yet the social boundaries remain remarkably resilient, with residential segregation in Belfast actually increasing in some neighborhoods even after the Good Friday Agreement supposedly brought peace. The echo has outlived the original sound, maintaining its destructive resonance even as the source has faded.

These religious echoes extend far beyond Ireland, manifesting in contexts that superficially appear unrelated to their historical origins. The Protestant work ethic that Max Weber identified as a cultural force shaping capitalism continues to influence attitudes toward labor, success, and moral worth in predominantly secular societies. The suspicion of hierarchy and the emphasis on individual conscience that emerged from the Protestant Reformation echo in contemporary American resistance to centralized authority and expert consensus, even among people with no connection to Protestant theology. Meanwhile, Catholic traditions of subsidiarity and communal solidarity inform approaches to social welfare and community organization, even as church attendance declines. These cultural echoes operate below the level of conscious religious belief, shaping intuitions about the proper organization of society, the relationship between individual and community, and the sources of moral authority. They create invisible fault lines in contemporary debates, where disagreements that appear to be about policy or pragmatics actually reflect deeper, older patterns of thought about the nature of the good society.

The economic echoes of historical divisions prove equally persistent and perhaps even more consequential for contemporary fragmentation. The Industrial Revolution created a chasm between capital and labor, between factory owners and workers, that structured political conflict for more than a century. The specific conditions of nineteenth-century industrial capitalism have long since evolved—child labor has been abolished in developed nations, unions have won basic protections, and the nature of work itself has transformed from manufacturing to services and information processing. Yet the fundamental identity division between those who own capital and those who sell their labor continues to structure political coalitions and shape policy debates. More importantly, the echo of this division has generated new variations that maintain the same basic pattern while adapting to changed circumstances. The gig economy creates a new class of workers who are simultaneously independent contractors and utterly dependent on platform companies, echoing the vulnerability of early industrial workers while lacking even the basic protections those workers eventually won. The financialization of the economy concentrates wealth in ways that echo the robber baron era, with hedge fund managers and private equity executives replacing railroad magnates and steel barons as the commanding heights of capitalism. Each generation believes it faces novel economic challenges. Yet, the underlying patterns of division between those who benefit from existing financial arrangements and those who bear the costs remain remarkably consistent.

These economic echoes intertwine with racial divisions, amplifying both. The particular horror of chattel slavery in the Americas created racial categories and hierarchies that reverberate through every contemporary discussion of inequality, justice, and opportunity. The wealth accumulated through slave labor funded the industrial development of Northern cities and the agricultural empire of the South, creating economic disparities that compound across generations through inheritance, social capital, and accumulated advantage. But the echo extends beyond mere economic inequality into the realm of identity and social status. The racial classifications created to justify slavery— the elaborate pseudoscientific theories of racial hierarchy, the one-drop rules designed to maintain clear boundaries, the social rituals of deference and domination—all continue to structure social interactions and shape life chances long after the formal legal apparatus of racial subordination has been dismantled. When contemporary debates about education policy, criminal justice, or urban development erupt into seemingly intractable conflict, they often amplify echoes of older divisions, with each side hearing different historical resonances in what appears, on the surface, to be a straightforward policy discussion.

The mechanisms by which these historical echoes propagate involve complex interactions among personal memory, institutional structures, and cultural narratives. At the individual level, family histories transmit not just stories but emotional orientations and social identities. A child who grows up hearing about how their ancestors were persecuted, displaced, or deprived develops a psychological framework that sensitizes them to similar patterns in their own experience, even when the specific forms of injustice have changed. This intergenerational transmission of trauma and grievance does not require deliberate indoctrination; it occurs through casual conversations, through patterns of trust and suspicion modeled by parents, through the emotional tone with which different groups are discussed. Research on epigenetics suggests that severe trauma may even create biological changes that are transmitted across generations, though the evidence for this in humans remains contested. What is beyond dispute is that the psychological and cultural transmission of historical experience shapes how people perceive threats, evaluate fairness, and determine who belongs to their moral community.

Institutional structures provide another crucial mechanism for propagating echoes of past divisions. Laws, once enacted, create constituencies invested in their continuation and establish precedents that constrain future possibilities. The boundaries drawn by historical gerrymandering continue to shape political representation long after the specific partisan advantage they were designed to create has shifted. Property rights established through historical dispossession—whether of Native Americans, Mexican landholders in the Southwest, or African Americans excluded from homeownership through redlining—create patterns of wealth inequality that persist across generations through inheritance and compound interest. Educational systems, shaped by historical battles over curriculum and control, transmit not just knowledge but particular ways of understanding national identity and social obligation. These institutional echoes are particularly insidious because they appear neutral and permanent, as though the arrangements they embody represent natural or inevitable features of social organization rather than contingent outcomes of historical conflicts.

Cultural narratives and collective memories constitute perhaps the most potent mechanism for propagating historical divisions into the present. Every society tells itself stories about its origins, its heroes, its triumphs, and its tragedies. These narratives provide frameworks for making sense of contemporary events and for determining who deserves sympathy, blame, reward, or punishment. In the United States, competing narratives about the nation's founding—whether it represents a revolutionary commitment to liberty and equality or a slaveholding republic built on indigenous dispossession—generate radically different implications for contemporary policy and social arrangements. The controversy over historical monuments provides a vivid illustration of how these competing narratives clash in public space. Confederate memorials erected during the Jim Crow era were designed to echo and reinforce a particular interpretation of the Civil War as a noble Lost Cause rather than a rebellion in defense of slavery. The echo they generate depends entirely on the listener's position: to some, they represent heritage and historical memory; to others, they symbolize ongoing intimidation and the celebration of treason and racial subjugation. Neither side can fully hear what the other hears in these echoes because they are listening from different positions in the chamber of history, with different accumulated experiences shaping their acoustic perception.

The amplification of historical echoes through modern communication technologies is a distinctive feature of contemporary division, distinguishing it from past iterations. In previous eras, historical grievances could fade somewhat as direct witnesses died and succeeding generations gained temporal and emotional distance from originating events. The attenuation of collective memory allowed for reconciliation and the gradual erosion of old enmities. Modern media disrupts this natural process of forgetting by making historical images, documents, and testimonies permanently and immediately accessible. The videos of police violence against Black Americans circulate endlessly on social media, ensuring that each new incident is viewed not as an isolated occurrence but as one more example in a long, documented pattern stretching back to slave patrols and lynch mobs. Similarly, every act of left-wing violence or property destruction is catalogued and shared among conservative communities as evidence of an ongoing threat stretching back to anarchist bombers and Communist revolutionaries. The digital archive prevents the fading of echoes; instead, they can be summoned instantly and played back at full volume whenever contemporary events seem to resonate with historical patterns. This creates a temporal collapse where past and present merge, making it psychologically difficult to distinguish between inherited grievances and immediate threats.

Social media algorithms exacerbate this amplification by serving content that resonates with users' existing historical narratives and emotional orientations. Someone whose social identity has been shaped by echoes of

21

historical victimization will be presented with endless evidence that the patterns persist. At the same time, alternative interpretations and counterexamples remain invisible or marginalized in their information environment. This creates echo chambers in both the metaphorical and literal sense—spaces where historical echoes reverberate without interference, building in intensity rather than gradually dissipating. The result is a society in which different communities live in fundamentally different historical realities, hearing completely different echoes from the same events. A Supreme Court decision on affirmative action echoes as a correction of historical injustice for some and as new discrimination for others; an immigration policy echoes as national self-preservation for some and as racism and xenophobia for others; a change in school curriculum echoes as inclusive education for some and as cultural obliteration for others.

The challenge of distinguishing between legitimate echoes that demand continued attention and destructive reverberations that prevent progress represents one of the most challenging problems in any reunification effort. Not all historical divisions should be forgotten or transcended; some contain crucial moral lessons, honor genuine sacrifices, and remind us of principles worth defending. The memory of the Holocaust must echo through time as a warning against the industrial application of hatred and the dangers of dehumanizing ideologies. The memory of the Civil Rights Movement must echo as an inspiration and a reminder of the courage required to challenge entrenched injustice. The memory of women's suffrage struggles must echo to honor the sacrifices made for rights now taken for granted and to remind us that progress is neither inevitable nor easily won. These are echoes worth preserving, amplifying, and transmitting across generations. The question becomes how to maintain the productive echoes that teach, inspire, and warn while damping the destructive reverberations that trap us in cycles of recrimination and prevent the formation of new solidarities.

This distinction cannot be made through abstract principle but requires careful attention to the effects that particular echoes produce in contemporary contexts. Productive echoes tend to expand moral imagination, increase empathy for others' experiences, and inspire action to address current injustices. They connect past struggles to present possibilities, showing that change is achievable and that ordinary people can make extraordinary contributions to justice. Destructive echoes, by contrast, tend to narrow moral community, justify present-day antagonism through past grievances, and create a sense of permanent victimhood or entitlement that immunizes one's own group from criticism. They use historical suffering to license contemporary cruelty or indifference, employing past injuries as weapons in current conflicts. The same historical event can generate both productive and destructive echoes depending on how its memory is deployed. The Holocaust can echo as a universal warning about the fragility of civilization and the importance of defending the vulnerable, or it can echo as a justification for visiting suffering on other people who are cast as perpetual threats. The difference lies not in the historical event itself but in the use to which its memory is put.

Breaking cycles of destructive echoes while preserving productive historical memory requires developing what might be called acoustic literacy—the ability to recognize when we are responding to echoes rather than to present realities, to trace those echoes back to their sources, and to make conscious decisions about which reverberations deserve amplification and which should be allowed to dissipate. This is not a matter of forgetting history or pretending that past injustices did not occur. Instead, it involves developing a more sophisticated relationship with historical memory, one that acknowledges both continuities and discontinuities between past and present, that recognizes how our inherited frameworks shape perception without being entirely determined by them, and that maintains openness to evidence that contradicts inherited narratives. Acoustic literacy means being able to say, "I understand why this situation triggers echoes of past persecution, but I need to examine whether the present circumstances actually parallel the past or whether the echo is distorting my perception." It means being willing to ask, "What am I not hearing because my positioning in the echo chamber makes certain sounds inaudible to me?"

The prospects for developing such acoustic literacy across society remain uncertain but not hopeless. Educational approaches that teach history in its full complexity—acknowledging both the genuinely heroic and the deeply shameful aspects of our collective past—can help people develop more nuanced relationships with historical echoes. When students learn that their ancestors were capable of both extraordinary courage and terrible cruelty, that simple narratives of perpetual victimization or unblemished heroism distort reality, they become less likely to use historical echoes as weapons and more likely to see them as invitations to reflection and growth. Shared commemorative practices that honor the full humanity of all parties to historical conflicts, that mourn all suffering while still making moral distinctions about responsibility and justice, can create spaces where different echoes are heard and acknowledged without requiring complete agreement about their interpretation. Most fundamentally, creating opportunities for people to form meaningful relationships across lines of historical division can help them recognize that the echoes they hear are not the only possible reverberations from past events, that others with different positions in the acoustic space hear something quite different, and that both sets of echoes may contain legitimate elements deserving consideration.

The work of dampening destructive echoes while preserving productive historical memory ultimately requires what scholars of collective memory call "agonistic remembrance"—a form of memory work that acknowledges ongoing conflicts over interpretation rather than seeking premature consensus or forced forgetting. This approach accepts that different communities will continue to hear different echoes from the same historical events. Still, it insists that these differences be engaged through dialogue rather than shouted across the divide. It means creating forums where people can share the echoes they hear, explain the experiences and inheritances that shape their acoustic perception, and work to understand what others hear, even when complete agreement remains impossible. The goal is not to eliminate historical echoes or achieve a single harmonious narrative, but to create a polyphonic social space where multiple echoes can coexist, where their conflicts and consonances are acknowledged, and where new compositions might emerge from the interaction of different reverberations.

The echoes of historical division that reverberate through contemporary society represent both a tremendous challenge and a potential resource for reunification. They are a challenge because they perpetuate conflicts across time, create hair-trigger sensitivities that can explode into open hostility, and make it challenging to evaluate present circumstances on their own merits rather than through the distorting lens of inherited grievances. But they are also a resource because they connect us to the struggles, sacrifices, and wisdom of previous generations. After all, they prevent the erasure of genuine injustices that demand continued attention, and they provide raw material for understanding how divisions emerge and persist over time. The question is not whether historical echoes will continue to shape our social landscape—they inevitably will—but whether we can develop the acoustic literacy necessary to distinguish productive from destructive reverberations, to honor genuine historical lessons while refusing to be imprisoned by past conflicts, and to create new harmonies that incorporate rather than suppress the dissonances of our shared history. This requires neither the impossible task of silencing all echoes nor the dangerous project of amplifying only those that serve current political purposes, but the complex, ongoing work of listening carefully to what history is still trying to tell us and making conscious choices about which echoes deserve our attention as we attempt to compose a more unified social symphony.

The temporal dimension of echoes deserves further consideration, particularly the ways they can create what historians call "temporal drag"—the phenomenon in which communities remain psychologically anchored to moments of historical trauma or triumph long after the objective conditions have changed. In Poland, the memory of the partitions that erased the nation from the map for over a century continues to generate intense anxiety about sovereignty and foreign influence, shaping contemporary responses to European Union integration and refugee policies in ways that puzzle outside observers who lack access to this historical resonance. The Polish wariness of external authority is not irrational xenophobia but an echo of genuine existential threats. Yet, this echo can prevent adaptive responses to genuinely novel situations that bear only superficial resemblance to past dangers. Similarly, the memory of hyperinflation in Weimar Germany continues to echo through German economic policy nearly a century later, creating fierce resistance to monetary expansion even in circumstances that differ fundamentally from the 1920s. These echoes anchor communities at particular historical moments, making it difficult to move forward even when clinging to past lessons becomes maladaptive.

The phenomenon of "echo entrepreneurs"—political and cultural leaders who deliberately amplify particular historical resonances for contemporary purposes—adds another layer of complexity to understanding how divisions perpetuate themselves. These actors recognize the emotional power of historical echoes and strategically invoke them to mobilize support, delegitimize opponents, or justify policies. When politicians compare vaccine mandates to the Holocaust or describe political opponents as fascists, they are not making careful historical arguments but rather attempting to trigger the mighty emotional echoes associated with those historical horrors. Such comparisons typically outrage those with different relationships to the referenced history, who hear the invocation as trivializing genuine suffering or weaponizing sacred memory. The promiscuous deployment of historical analogies—everything becomes "just like" some past atrocity or triumph—degrades our collective ability to distinguish between situations that genuinely parallel historical patterns and those that merely share superficial features. This echo inflation creates a boy-who-cried-wolf problem, making it harder to recognize genuine historical parallels because the acoustic space has been polluted with false resonances.

Yet echo entrepreneurs succeed because they tap into real reverberations rather than creating them from nothing. A demagogue cannot manufacture historical echoes in populations with no memory of the events being invoked; they can only amplify echoes that already exist in the social soundscape. This suggests that countering destructive amplification requires not just calling out cynical manipulation but addressing the underlying historical experiences and inherited narratives that make specific populations susceptible to particular appeals. When economic anxiety makes working-class communities vulnerable to scapegoating narratives, the solution is not simply to condemn the scapegoating but to address the genuine economic dislocations that make historical echoes of past financial crises resonate so powerfully. When minority communities remain vigilant against threats to hard-won rights, dismissing their concerns as paranoia or living in the past ignores how recent many historical injustices actually are and how fragile legal protections can prove when political winds shift. The echoes persist because the conditions that created them have not been fully resolved, and new reverberations continue to be generated by ongoing inequalities and injustices that bear family resemblances to historical patterns.

The international dimension of historical echoes adds further complications to reunification efforts. Historical divisions within nations increasingly resonate with global conflicts and ideological competition, creating what might be called "harmonic interference," in which domestic echoes align with and amplify international reverberations. The American culture wars increasingly echo the broader Western conflicts over liberalism, tradition, and identity, with each domestic skirmish understood as part of a civilizational struggle rather than a local dispute. Conservative media frames progressive cultural changes as echoing European decline and socialist collapse, while progressive media frames conservative resistance as echoing global authoritarian movements and fascist resurgence. These international harmonics make domestic reconciliation more difficult because local conflicts become invested with global significance, and domestic opponents become representatives of threatening international forces rather than fellow citizens with different views. The echo chamber becomes global, with reverberations crossing borders and returning transformed but intensified, making it impossible to address domestic divisions in isolation from broader international patterns.

Chapter 3: A Journey Through Dialogue

The restoration of genuine conversation represents perhaps the most fundamental challenge in reunifying a fractured society, yet it is also the most immediate and actionable pathway available to us. While we have examined the structural forces that divide us and the historical patterns that amplify our separations, the work of reconnection ultimately happens in the intimate spaces where human beings encounter one another through words, presence, and mutual attention. Dialogue—authentic, sustained, and intentional—serves as the primary vehicle through which abstract others become concrete individuals, through which ideological opponents become complex human beings, and through which the possibility of shared understanding emerges from the fog of mutual suspicion. This chapter explores not the theory of dialogue but its practice, the actual journey that individuals and communities undertake when they commit to conversing across the chasms that divide them, complete with all the false starts, uncomfortable silences, unexpected breakthroughs, and gradual transformations that characterize this profoundly human endeavor.

The first obstacle encountered on any journey through dialogue is not disagreement but the profound discomfort of beginning. In contemporary society, we have developed elaborate mechanisms for avoiding genuine conversation with those we perceive as different or opposed to us. We curate our social environments, both physical and digital, to minimize encounters with perspectives that challenge our assumptions. We have perfected the art of parallel monologue, where groups of like-minded individuals take turns expressing their views without ever truly engaging with alternative perspectives. The prospect of intentionally seeking out such engagement triggers anxiety that operates on multiple levels. There is the fear of being changed by the encounter, of having our certainties destabilized by information or perspectives we cannot easily dismiss. There is the fear of being judged or condemned, of having our most fundamental values characterized as evidence of moral failure. There is the social fear of being seen by our own communities as consorting with the enemy, of having our loyalty questioned for choosing to humanize rather than demonize. Before any productive dialogue can occur, individuals must find the courage to move through these fears, acknowledging them honestly rather than pretending they do not exist. The journey begins not with eloquent words but with the simple, vulnerable decision to show up and attempt connection despite profound discomfort.

Those who have facilitated dialogue across deep divides consistently observe a predictable initial phase characterized by what might be called "performative positioning." Participants enter the conversation space carrying invisible banners that declare their tribal affiliations and ideological commitments. Their initial contributions to the dialogue serve primarily to establish these identities rather than to explore genuine curiosity about the other. A conservative participant might begin by establishing credentials through references to traditional values and skepticism of government overreach. A progressive participant might lead with affirmations of social justice priorities and acknowledgment of systemic oppression. These opening gambits are not insincere, but they are primarily defensive, designed to ensure that the participant is not mistaken for something they are not, that their core identity remains intact and visible throughout whatever follows. Skilled facilitators recognize this phase as necessary rather than problematic. The performative positioning serves an important psychological function, creating a secure base from which participants can eventually venture into more uncertain territory. Attempting to short-circuit this phase by immediately demanding vulnerability or challenging cherished positions typically backfires, reinforcing defensiveness rather than dissolving it. The journey through dialogue requires patience with these initial rituals of identity establishment, understanding them as the natural precondition for whatever genuine exchange might follow.

A crucial transition occurs when the conversation shifts from abstract categories to concrete experiences. This shift often happens through the simple act of storytelling, when participants move beyond position statements to share narratives from their own lives that illuminate how they came to hold particular views or why specific issues matter deeply to them. A rural conservative might share the story of watching their community's economic foundation crumble as industries departed, describing the shame of unemployment, the dissolution of neighborhoods, and the sense that distant urban elites cared nothing for their suffering. A young progressive activist might recount experiences of discrimination, describing not just abstract injustice but specific moments of humiliation, fear, or exclusion that made activism feel like a moral imperative rather than a political preference. These stories have transformative power because they bypass the usual ideological defenses. It becomes far more difficult to dismiss someone as brainwashed or morally deficient when you have heard them describe, in specific and vulnerable terms, the experiences that shaped their perspective. The stories reveal the human being beneath the political label, demonstrating that even views we find abhorrent or incomprehensible are typically rooted in some recognizable human experience— fear, loss, aspiration, or loyalty. The journey through dialogue accelerates dramatically when participants discover that their opponents' views, however much they may disagree with them, emerge from the exact basic human needs and experiences that animate their own commitments.

Yet storytelling alone does not constitute sufficient dialogue, and communities that rely exclusively on narrative sharing without moving toward genuine engagement with differences often find themselves stuck in a comfortable but ultimately stagnant place. There is a seductive quality to the "we all have stories" approach, which can create an artificial harmony that avoids rather than addresses fundamental disagreements. Two people can share moving personal narratives, feel genuine empathy for each other's experiences, and remain in absolute opposition on critical questions of policy, justice, or social organization. The next phase of the journey requires participants to risk something more challenging than vulnerability—they must risk genuine disagreement while maintaining connection. This means learning to articulate not just "I believe X" but "I believe X, and here is why I think your contrary belief leads to outcomes that concern me." It means developing the capacity to challenge another person's logic, evidence, or conclusions while simultaneously communicating respect for their humanity and genuine interest in understanding their response to the challenge. This is among the most difficult skills in human interaction, requiring the simultaneous engagement of multiple capacities that do not naturally coexist: intellectual rigor and emotional attunement, commitment to truth and generosity of interpretation, willingness to push hard, and willingness to be pushed in return. Many dialogue initiatives founder at precisely this point, either retreating to safe sharing that avoids substantive disagreement or collapsing into argumentation that sacrifices connection for the satisfaction of scoring points.

The communities and organizations that have achieved remarkable success in sustaining dialogue across profound differences share a common practice: they cultivate what might be called "metabolic patience." This term captures the recognition that genuine understanding and relationship transformation operate on biological rather than mechanical timelines. Just as the body requires time to process nutrients, convert them into energy, and build new tissue, the human psyche requires extended time to process challenging information, integrate new perspectives, and construct new understandings. Our contemporary culture, with its emphasis on efficiency and immediate results, has largely lost touch with this fundamental reality. We expect insight to arrive instantaneously, positions to shift after a single conversation, and reconciliation to follow immediately upon the recognition of misunderstanding. But the practitioners of dialogue know differently. They observe that the most significant shifts in understanding typically occur not during the conversation itself but in the days and weeks following, as participants unconsciously work through what they heard, notice things in their own lives that suddenly seem relevant to perspectives they encountered, or find themselves unexpectedly defending an opponent's position to members of their own tribe. The journey through dialogue is not a sprint or even a marathon but something more like a pilgrimage, where the destination remains distant and the value lies as much in the transformation that occurs during the journey as in any eventual arrival.

Essential to sustaining this patient journey is the development of what researchers in conflict resolution call "dialogical infrastructure"—the social and institutional structures that support ongoing conversation rather than one-time encounters—the limitations of single-event dialogue become apparent when we consider the typical arc of such interactions. Strangers from opposing tribes gather, share stories, experience unexpected connections, and perhaps even gain genuine insights into each other's perspectives. Then they return to their respective communities, where all the forces that initially created division continue to operate. Without sustained connection and ongoing dialogue, the insights fade, the empathy dissipates, and within weeks the encounter becomes merely a pleasant memory rather than a transformative experience. In contrast, communities that create infrastructure for sustained dialogue—regular meeting spaces, established norms for engagement, rotating facilitators, deliberate integration with other community activities—enable something qualitatively different. Participants develop genuine relationships that survive disagreement. They build shared histories of successfully navigating conflict together. They create reputations within their own tribes as people who bridge divides, potentially licensing others to attempt similar journeys. The infrastructure transforms dialogue from an event into a practice, from an experiment into a way of life.

The role of physical space in supporting dialogue proves far more significant than most digital-age observers initially recognize. While online platforms offer convenience and can connect people across vast geographical distances, they lack crucial elements that facilitate the kind of dialogue that transforms relationships. The absence of physical presence removes numerous subtle channels of communication—body language, tone of voice, the tiny hesitations and accelerations that signal uncertainty or passion, the shared experience of occupying a common space. More fundamentally, digital communication lacks what might be called "escape friction." In face-to-face dialogue, leaving requires a deliberate physical action— standing up and walking out—that most social norms constrain us from performing, except in extreme circumstances. This mild constraint proves valuable because it keeps participants engaged through moments of discomfort that, if easily escaped, would prevent breakthrough. Online, the exit is always one click away, and the temptation to flee discomfort often proves irresistible.

Communities committed to dialogue have rediscovered the importance of carefully designed physical spaces—rooms arranged to facilitate eye contact without confrontation, comfortable enough to encourage relaxation but not so comfortable that people disengage, with elements like food or drink that provide natural breaks and opportunities for informal interaction. The journey through dialogue requires bodies in space, not merely minds connected through screens.

A compelling dimension of dialogue that deserves detailed attention is the phenomenon of "reciprocal revelation"—the process by which participants gradually discover that their opponents struggle with similar internal conflicts and ambivalences. The political and media ecosystem encourages us to present ourselves as certain about every issue aligned with our tribal identity. Conservatives must oppose every aspect of the progressive agenda without reservation; progressives must embrace every item in the social justice catalogue without nuance. But nearly every human being actually holds a complex mix of views, experiences uncertainties and doubts, and recognizes tensions between different values they hold. The small-government conservative may nonetheless believe that some market failures require government intervention. The progressive activist may harbor private doubts about particular tactics or claims within their movement. In sustained dialogue, as trust develops, participants begin to share these internal complexities, often hesitantly and with apparent guilt about their "impure" thoughts. What they discover, almost invariably, is that their opponents experience similar complexity. The pro-life advocate admits to understanding why someone might choose abortion in devastating circumstances. The abortion rights supporter acknowledges discomfort with late-term procedures. These mutual revelations of complexity do not necessarily lead to agreement, but they fundamentally alter the nature of disagreement. The other is no longer a monolithic enemy but a fellow human being navigating moral complexity, balancing competing values, and doing their best to arrive at defensible positions in a genuinely challenging landscape. The journey through dialogue leads not to the elimination of difference but to the recognition that difference emerges from processes of reasoning and feeling that both parties share.

      The question of scale presents one of the most challenging practical problems for those seeking to use dialogue as a tool for social reunification. Face-to-face dialogue, particularly the intensive sustained variety that produces genuine transformation, inevitably involves relatively small numbers of people. A dialogue group that grows beyond twenty or thirty participants loses the intimacy necessary for vulnerability and the equality of voice required for genuine exchange. Yet the divisions plaguing contemporary society operate on a scale of millions or hundreds of millions. How can intimate dialogue at a small scale contribute meaningfully to reunification at a societal scale? The answer lies not in scaling dialogue itself but in understanding how dialogue participants become carriers of transformed understanding within their broader communities. When someone embarks on a journey through dialogue, they return to their regular social networks—families, workplaces, religious communities, friend groups—as somewhat different people. They respond to conversations about politics or social issues with more nuance, resist simplistic demonization of the other side, share stories of actual people they have met who hold different views, and model the possibility of maintaining both conviction and connection. They become what network theorists call "bridging nodes," individuals positioned at the intersection of otherwise separate social networks who can transmit information, norms, and practices between groups. The impact of dialogue scales not through mass participation but through the social influence of those who participate, as their transformed understanding ripples outward through the multiple networks they inhabit. A single person who engages in genuine dialogue across differences might directly influence dozens of family members, friends, and colleagues, who, in turn, affect their networks, creating expanding waves of transformed understanding.

Failure represents an essential aspect of the dialogue journey that deserves honest examination. Not every dialogue succeeds. Not every conversation produces a breakthrough. Some encounters that begin with hope and good intentions end in renewed hostility and a more profound conviction that the other side is irredeemable. Understanding the nature and causes of dialogue failure proves as necessary as celebrating the successes. Some failures result from inadequate preparation or facilitation— participants lacking the basic skills of active listening, facilitators unable to intervene constructively when conversation becomes destructive, or groups attempting dialogue without establishing explicit norms and shared expectations. Other failures stem from wrong timing, attempting dialogue when participants are too freshly wounded or too deeply threatened to access the resources needed for genuine engagement. Still other failures emerge when the underlying power dynamics are too unbalanced, when one party to the dialogue faces existential threats that the other does not, making the seeming symmetry of dialogue itself a form of injustice. A productive approach to failure recognizes it as information rather than proof of impossibility. Failed dialogues can teach us about necessary preconditions, help identify what forms of hurt run too deep for immediate reconciliation, and clarify which conflicts require resolution through mechanisms other than conversation. The journey through dialogue is not a universal solvent that addresses every division, but a powerful tool whose limits we must understand as clearly as its possibilities.

The relationship between dialogue and action poses a tension that participants frequently struggle to navigate. Does commitment to ongoing dialogue require suspending activism, setting aside vigorous advocacy for policies and changes one believes necessary? Or can dialogue and activism coexist, and if so, under what conditions? This question proves particularly acute for members of communities that experience ongoing harm from current arrangements. A person facing discrimination, economic marginalization, or a threat to their fundamental rights may reasonably question whether they should invest time in understanding their oppressor's perspective rather than organizing to resist oppression. The resolution of this tension lies not in choosing between dialogue and action but in recognizing them as complementary strategies suited to different aspects of social transformation. Dialogue proves essential for changing hearts and minds, for building the coalitions necessary to sustain change, and for crafting solutions that address underlying needs rather than merely securing temporary advantage. Activism and advocacy prove essential for creating the urgency that makes dialogue possible, for protecting vulnerable communities during the extended timelines that transformation requires, and for demonstrating the seriousness of commitment to change. Communities successfully navigating the journey through dialogue often maintain both dialogical spaces, where respectful engagement across difference is the norm, and advocacy spaces, where passionate argument and political organizing proceed without the constraints of dialogue. The key lies in preventing dialogue from becoming an excuse for inaction and preventing activism from degenerating into demonization that makes eventual reconciliation impossible.

The transformation that dialogue produces in participants operates at multiple levels simultaneously, from the intellectual to the emotional to the almost spiritual. Intellectually, participants in sustained dialogue typically develop a more sophisticated understanding of the issues that divide them, recognizing complexities and tradeoffs they had not previously considered. Emotionally, they experience the humanization of the other, the replacement of the abstract enemy with a concrete individual whose fears and hopes become partially visible. But many participants describe a more profound shift, harder to articulate—a change in their basic orientation toward difference itself. Before dialogue, differences felt threatening, a challenge to their understanding of truth and justice that required either conversion or condemnation of the other. After sustained dialogue, difference becomes more like an inevitable feature of human diversity, something to be engaged and worked with rather than eliminated. This shift does not mean abandoning conviction or embracing relativism. Participants still believe their own views are correct and essential. But they hold these beliefs with what might be called "humble confidence," secure in their own perspective while remaining genuinely curious about how others see things differently. This reorientation toward difference may represent dialogue's most important contribution to social reunification, as it addresses not just specific disagreements but the underlying psychological stances that make those disagreements feel intolerable.

The emerging field of "dialogue training" reveals that the capacities needed for productive conversation across difference can be systematically developed through practice and instruction. These capacities include active listening, the ability to genuinely hear what another person is saying without immediately formulating counter-arguments; empathic imagination, the skill of temporarily inhabiting another person's perspective to understand how the world looks from their vantage point; cognitive complexity, the capacity to hold multiple perspectives simultaneously and recognize validity in positions one ultimately disagrees with; emotional regulation, the ability to manage one's own triggered responses sufficiently to remain engaged rather than attacking or withdrawing; and dialogical courage, the willingness to risk being changed by what one hears. None of these capacities comes naturally to most people, especially in contemporary environments that actively work against their development. Social media platforms reward quick reactions over careful thought, partisan media ecosystems model contempt rather than curiosity, and the pace of modern life leaves little space for the kind of extended reflection that dialogue requires. But experiments in schools, universities, religious institutions, and civic organizations demonstrate that these capacities can be taught and strengthened through deliberate practice. Teaching dialogue is itself a form of social reunification, as it equips the rising generation with tools the current generation largely lacks.

The relationship between personal transformation and structural change represents the final frontier in understanding dialogue's role in social reunification. Critics of dialogue initiatives often charge that conversation serves as a substitute for action, directing energy that should go toward changing unjust systems into therapeutic exercises that make privileged people feel better without changing anything fundamental. This critique contains an important truth—dialogue alone cannot transform institutions, redistribute power, or dismantle structures of oppression. No amount of heartfelt conversation will close racial wealth gaps, reverse environmental destruction, or reform political systems that channel power to the already powerful. Yet dismissing dialogue as merely personal rather than political misunderstands the relationship between individual consciousness and social structure. Structural changes, even when achieved through political pressure or social movement victories, prove fragile if they lack supporting shifts in public understanding and relationships. Desegregation laws did not end racism because structural integration, unaccompanied by transformed human relationships, often replicated exclusion through new mechanisms. Conversely, transformed consciousness that develops through genuine dialogue creates conditions in which structural reforms become possible, as people who have journeyed together across their differences prove more willing to support policies that reduce advantage for their own group in the service of greater justice. The most profound social transformations require both structural reform and relational healing, both policy change and consciousness shift, both institutional redesign and the patient journey through dialogue that enables former adversaries to recognize their shared stake in a reunified society.

The journey through dialogue ultimately offers not a destination but a practice, not a solution but a pathway. In deeply divided societies, no conversation will eliminate fundamental disagreements about justice, truth, or the proper organization of social life. What dialogue offers is the possibility of holding these disagreements within a larger context of mutual recognition and continued relationship. It demonstrates that we can disagree profoundly while acknowledging each other's humanity, that we can advocate fiercely for our own positions while remaining genuinely curious about what we might be missing, and that we can build enough trust to work together on shared challenges despite lacking consensus on ultimate questions. The practice of dialogue, sustained over years and embedded in communities, gradually weaves new threads into the social fabric, not replacing old divisions with homogeneity but creating stronger, more flexible connections that hold diverse parts together in productive tension. This journey requires courage to begin, patience to sustain, and humility to accept that transformation follows timelines we do not control, but for societies seeking reunification without uniformity, for communities pursuing connection without erasure of difference, the journey through dialogue remains our most human and most hopeful path forward.

Chapter 4: Bridging the Divide

The metaphor of bridging contains within it a profound truth about the nature of reunification: we do not eliminate the distances that separate us, nor do we pretend they do not exist. Instead, we construct pathways across them, creating connections that acknowledge difference while enabling movement, exchange, and mutual access. Having explored the structural fractures in our social fabric, the historical echoes that amplify division, and the conversational pathways that enable reconnection, we must now turn our attention to the practical architecture of bridge-building itself—the specific strategies, structures, and approaches that transform theoretical possibilities into lived realities. This work demands more than good intentions or wishful thinking; it requires understanding the engineering principles of social connection, the materials that withstand stress, and the maintenance practices that prevent decay. The bridges we must construct span chasms carved by decades of increasing polarization, reinforced by algorithmic sorting, and widened by economic anxieties and cultural dislocations. Yet throughout history, human societies have demonstrated a remarkable capacity to build such connections even across seemingly unbridgeable divides, and the lessons from these successful efforts illuminate the path forward for our own fractured moment.

The first principle of effective bridge-building involves recognizing that sustainable connections cannot be imposed from above or engineered through top-down mandates alone. The most durable bridges in divided societies emerge from what might be called "the middle space"—that crucial realm where civil society organizations, local community leaders, religious institutions, professional associations, and informal networks operate with relative autonomy from both governmental control and pure market forces. This middle space has been progressively hollowed out in many contemporary societies, as hyperpartisanship has colonized institutions that once maintained political neutrality, as economic pressures have undermined organizations that depended on membership dues rather than foundation grants or corporate sponsorship, and as digital platforms have replaced physical gathering places where diverse people encountered one another organically. Rebuilding this middle space requires deliberate effort and resources, but also protection from the forces that would subordinate every institution to partisan purposes. Professional associations that once brought together people of diverse political views around shared vocational concerns must resist pressure to make partisan pronouncements on every contemporary controversy. Universities must preserve spaces where intellectual exploration proceeds according to scholarly standards rather than ideological litmus tests. Religious institutions must remember that their ultimate loyalties transcend temporal political divisions. Labor unions, business groups, civic clubs, and recreational organizations all perform bridging functions when they create contexts where shared activities and common purposes take precedence over the political identities that might otherwise keep people apart.

A crucial insight from successful bridge-building efforts concerns the importance of "contact theory" while simultaneously recognizing its limitations and necessary conditions. Social psychological research has long established that contact between members of different groups can reduce prejudice and increase empathy, but only under specific circumstances: the groups must have equal status within the contact situation, they must work toward common goals, their interaction must involve intergroup cooperation rather than competition, and the contact must receive support from relevant authorities and social norms.

When these conditions are met, cross-group friendships and positive associations can indeed form, changing attitudes and behaviors in ways that ripple outward into broader communities. However, contact under unfavorable conditions—where status hierarchies are reinforced, where competition is emphasized, where interactions confirm negative stereotypes—can actually increase prejudice and deepen divisions. This means that bridge-building initiatives must carefully structure the contexts in which encounters occur, creating frameworks that emphasize collaboration, distribute authority equitably, and establish norms of mutual respect. The success of specific integrated military units, diverse work teams focused on complex problem-solving, and community projects that bring together residents from segregated neighborhoods demonstrates that properly structured contact can indeed bridge divides, but the key lies in the careful attention to the conditions that make positive outcomes possible rather than assuming that mere proximity automatically generates understanding.

The concept of "bridging capital" provides another essential framework for understanding how to construct connections across social divides. Social capital theorists distinguish between "bonding capital"—the connections within homogeneous groups that provide solidarity, emotional support, and resource sharing among similar people—and "bridging capital"—the connections across diverse groups that give access to different resources, information, and perspectives. Contemporary society suffers from an oversupply of bonding capital within increasingly insular groups, combined with a severe deficit of bridging capital that connects them. This imbalance creates echo chambers where information and perspectives circulate only within like-minded communities, where social trust exists within groups but not between them, and where collective action can be mobilized for tribal purposes but not for everyday goods that require cross-group cooperation.

Rebuilding bridging capital requires creating and supporting institutions, organizations, and practices that inherently bring diverse people together around purposes that transcend their differences. Community colleges, which educate students from diverse socioeconomic and cultural backgrounds, serve this bridging function by fostering interaction across these differences. Mixed-income housing developments can generate bridging capital when designed to promote interaction rather than simply placing different groups in proximity. Youth sports leagues, community theaters, volunteer fire departments, and countless other local institutions have historically served as bridging infrastructure, and their revitalization represents a practical strategy for social reunification.

The role of economic cooperation in bridge-building deserves particular attention, as shared economic interests have historically provided powerful motivations for overcoming other sources of division. Worker cooperatives that give employees ownership stakes create situations in which people from diverse backgrounds must collaborate effectively to ensure their collective success. Regional economic development initiatives that require collaboration across jurisdictional boundaries generate incentives for political leaders to work together despite partisan differences. Industry associations that bring together companies facing common challenges create contexts where business leaders focus on shared concerns rather than political disagreements. The challenge in contemporary society is that economic changes have undermined many traditional institutions of economic cooperation while creating new forms of economic relationships that often increase rather than decrease social distance. The shift from manufacturing to service employment has eliminated workplaces where people of varied educational backgrounds worked side by side, replacing them with more homogeneous work environments sorted by credentials. The rise of the gig economy has atomized workers who might previously have developed solidarity through shared employment. The increasing geographic concentration of economic opportunity has created disparities that fuel resentment and political division. Addressing these trends requires conscious effort to develop new institutions of economic cooperation that can serve bridging functions—employee ownership structures that cross class lines, regional compacts that link prosperous metro areas with struggling rural regions, training programs that bring together people from different backgrounds around shared skill development, and economic policies that distribute opportunity widely enough to reduce the zero-sum thinking that fuels division.

Educational institutions represent particularly crucial sites for bridge-building because they shape the attitudes, skills, and social networks of successive generations. Schools that bring together students from diverse backgrounds, when they actively cultivate cross-group friendships and collaborative learning rather than allowing de facto segregation within nominally integrated institutions, can interrupt the reproduction of division across generations. Yet this potential is realized only when educational approaches actively promote bridging rather than inadvertently reinforcing separation. Tracking systems that sort students by academic performance often correlate with race and class, recreating segregation within diverse schools. Curriculum choices that emphasize grievances and identity categories without also building familiar narratives and shared purposes can heighten group consciousness without fostering connection. Extracurricular activities that self-select along demographic lines prevent the formation of cross-cutting ties. Effective educational bridge-building requires deliberate strategies: structured classroom cooperation that requires students of different backgrounds to work interdependently toward common goals, curricula that acknowledge historical injuries while also highlighting stories of successful collaboration and shared achievement, extracurricular activities designed to attract diverse participants, and teacher training that equips educators to facilitate difficult conversations while maintaining learning environments where all students feel respected and included. Higher education faces similar challenges and opportunities, with the additional complexity that students increasingly sort themselves into institutions that reflect their political and cultural identities, with conservative and progressive students attending different colleges and studying other subjects. Reversing this trend requires universities to cultivate intellectual diversity actively, to protect genuine academic freedom against pressure from both progressive activists and conservative politicians, and to emphasize the distinctive educational value of engaging seriously with perspectives that challenge one's assumptions.

Media ecosystems present both obstacles to bridge-building and potential pathways for connection, depending on how they are structured and utilized. The fragmentation of media audiences into separate information universes represents one of the most significant barriers to reunification, as people literally inhabit different factual realities and lack shared reference points for discussion. Yet media can also serve bridging functions when it provides platforms where different perspectives encounter one another in constructive ways, where complex issues receive nuanced treatment that resists binary thinking, and where accuracy and fairness take precedence over engagement metrics optimized for outrage. Public broadcasting, when adequately resourced and protected from political interference, has historically served this bridging function by providing news and cultural programming that appeals to diverse audiences and maintains professional standards of accuracy and balance. Local journalism, though severely diminished by economic pressures, plays a crucial role in creating shared narratives and common knowledge within communities, and its revitalization through new funding models represents an essential investment in social infrastructure. Beyond traditional media, digital platforms could be redesigned to promote bridging rather than division through interface changes that expose users to diverse perspectives, algorithmic adjustments that prioritize accuracy and nuance over engagement, and moderation policies that eliminate the most toxic behavior while preserving space for genuine disagreement. Some promising experiments involve "bridging-based ranking" systems that elevate content that people across political divides find valuable, "considered responses" that require users to pause before posting emotionally charged content, and "perspective-taking" features that help users understand how people with different backgrounds and beliefs might receive their messages.

The physical design of communities and public spaces profoundly influences the possibilities for bridge-building, though these spatial dimensions of social connection often receive insufficient attention. Urban planning and architectural choices determine whether people of different backgrounds encounter one another in daily life or remain isolated in separate bubbles. Suburban development patterns that eliminate public spaces and walkable streets reduce casual encounters among neighbors. At the same time, urban designs that include parks, libraries, community centers, and mixed-use districts create opportunities for interaction across lines of difference. The privatization of formerly public spaces—the replacement of town squares and public parks with shopping malls and gated communities—has eliminated venues where diverse citizens mingled as equals, replacing them with commercial spaces that sort people by purchasing power and lifestyle preferences. Reversing these trends requires urban design reforms that prioritize shared public spaces over private enclaves, zoning changes that encourage mixed-use and mixed-income neighborhoods rather than homogeneous subdivisions, and investments in public infrastructure that serve as gathering spaces for entire communities rather than particular segments. Successful examples include public markets that bring together residents of different backgrounds around food and commerce, waterfront developments that include extensive public access rather than exclusive residential towers, and transit-oriented development that increases interaction among people following different daily routines. Even seemingly minor design choices matter: benches that face one another rather than all pointing the same direction encourage conversation between strangers, community gardens that include shared spaces alongside individual plots promote cooperation, and public art installations that invite participation create opportunities for collective experience across lines of difference.

Religious institutions and spiritual practices offer distinctive resources for bridge-building, though religious difference itself represents a significant dimension of contemporary social fracture. Faith communities have historically served as sites of bonding capital within particular groups. Still, many religious traditions also emphasize hospitality to strangers, common humanity across apparent differences, and ultimate loyalties that transcend worldly divisions. When religious institutions and leaders emphasize these bridge-building dimensions of their traditions rather than weaponizing religious identity for political purposes, they can play influential roles in social reunification. Interfaith dialogue initiatives that bring together leaders and laypeople from different religious communities around shared concerns—such as poverty alleviation, environmental stewardship, addiction recovery, or community safety—create contexts in which participants discover common values despite theological differences. Faith-based community organizing that unites congregations across denominational and even interfaith lines to address local issues demonstrates that religious motivation can fuel civic cooperation rather than division. Religious institutions that maintain prophetic distance from partisan politics, criticizing injustice while refusing to become instruments of political parties, preserve the authority to call believers across political divides to higher loyalties and common purposes. The challenge involves navigating genuine theological differences and deeply felt moral convictions without either demanding theological uniformity or pretending that differences are trivial. The successful models tend to emphasize "competing together" rather than seeking agreement—accepting that people will continue to disagree about ultimate questions while finding ways to cooperate on practical matters and to extend mutual respect despite profound differences.

The arts and cultural production represent underutilized resources for bridge-building, capable of fostering empathy and understanding in ways that rational argument alone cannot achieve. Literature that illuminates the inner lives of people unlike ourselves cultivates imagination and perspective-taking, essential for crossing social divides. Theater that brings together performers and audiences from segregated communities creates a shared experience and reveals common humanity beneath surface differences. Music that draws on multiple cultural traditions demonstrates how diversity can be a source of creative richness rather than only conflict. Visual arts that address social divisions can make visible what has been overlooked, complicate simplistic narratives, and create spaces for reflection that propaganda and polemic foreclose. Community arts programs that bring together diverse participants as co-creators rather than passive consumers generate bridging capital through collaborative creative work. Cultural institutions, from museums to symphony orchestras to public libraries, can serve bridging functions when they make themselves genuinely accessible to entire communities rather than catering to elite segments, when their programming reflects diverse perspectives and experiences rather than a monoculture, and when they create opportunities for interaction and dialogue rather than merely presenting finished products for consumption. The key is moving beyond the "representation" model, which includes diverse voices, to a genuine "co-creation" model where people from different backgrounds collaborate in cultural production and interpretation, developing relationships and understanding through shared creative work.

Generational dynamics in bridge-building warrant particular attention, as different age cohorts relate to contemporary divisions in distinctive ways that both complicate and illuminate paths toward reunification. Younger generations have come of age in an era of heightened polarization and tend to be more sorted into separate political and cultural tribes than their parents or grandparents. Yet they also demonstrate greater comfort with diversity across many dimensions and less attachment to specific traditional sources of division. This paradox— simultaneous intensification of some divisions and relaxation of others—suggests that bridge-building strategies must be tailored to different generational contexts rather than assuming uniform approaches will work across age groups. For older adults, appeals to memory of less polarized times and institutions that once brought diverse people together may resonate, while younger people respond to different frames and approaches. Intergenerational bridge-building—creating contexts where various age groups work together toward common purposes—represents a particularly promising strategy because generational differences often cross-cut other lines of division, creating opportunities to disrupt the alignment of all identities along a single axis of conflict. Mentorship programs, oral history projects, intergenerational housing arrangements, and community service initiatives that unite young and old around shared work all build bridges that can make other divisions less salient and create alliance patterns that destabilize binary thinking.

The maintenance dimension of bridge-building—the ongoing work required to sustain connections once established—receives far less attention than the initial construction of bridges. Yet, this sustained effort determines whether bridging initiatives produce lasting change or merely temporary exceptions to prevailing patterns of division. Bridges require ongoing maintenance against the forces that would erode them: the gravitational pull of tribal identity, the friction generated by genuine disagreement, the weathering effects of national political polarization, and the simple entropy that affects all human institutions. Successful bridge-building initiatives include mechanisms for regular renewal and repair: routines that bring diverse participants together consistently rather than sporadically, conflict resolution processes that address tensions before they metastasize, leadership development that ensures bridging work continues as founding leaders move on, and evaluation approaches that assess relationship quality and institutional health rather than merely counting outputs. The metaphor of ecological restoration proves apt—like restored ecosystems that require ongoing management against invasive species and changing conditions, bridged communities require sustained attention and adaptation to remain healthy. This maintenance work is less dramatic than launching new initiatives and less likely to attract media coverage or foundation funding. Yet it is essential to translate temporary bridging episodes into permanent social infrastructure.

The relationship between local and national dynamics in bridge-building presents a persistent challenge, as successful connection-building at the community level often faces headwinds from national political polarization that incentivizes division. Local bridge-building initiatives can create spaces where national divisions seem less relevant and where practical cooperation proceeds despite differences, yet participants in these local efforts remain embedded in national media environments and political systems that constantly reinforce us-versus-them thinking. This tension means that local bridge-building, while necessary, is not sufficient for social reunification—we also need national-level changes in media systems, political institutions, and public discourse that support rather than undermine local bridging work. The relationship should be reciprocal: local successes demonstrating that cooperation across differences is possible and productive, creating models and momentum for national change. In contrast, national reforms create more favorable conditions for local bridging. This requires strategic thinking about how local initiatives can be scaled and connected, how successful models can be adapted to different contexts rather than merely replicated, and how grassroots bridge-building can inform and pressure for national institutional reforms. Networks that connect local bridging initiatives, share lessons, coordinate advocacy for supportive policies, and amplify voices calling for reunification can help translate dispersed local efforts into a broader movement capable of influencing national dynamics.

Ultimately, the project of bridging divides to reunify society requires a combination of structural reform, cultural change, and personal commitment that must be sustained over years and decades rather than months or single election cycles. No single initiative or approach suffices—we need simultaneous efforts across multiple levels and domains, from redesigning algorithms and reforming electoral systems to changing urban planning priorities and revitalizing community institutions. We need both broad societal shifts and countless individual decisions to reach across divides in daily life. The work is difficult precisely because it swims against powerful currents of polarization, sorting, and tribalism that have been building for decades and that serve the interests of various actors who benefit from division. Yet human history demonstrates repeatedly that even deeply divided societies can bridge their differences when enough people commit to the work, when leaders emerge who prioritize unity over partisan advantage, when institutions are reformed to reward bridge-building rather than division, and when cultural narratives shift from emphasizing what separates us to recognizing what we share. The bridges we need will not build themselves, but neither are they impossible to construct. They require the patient, sustained effort of people willing to span chasms, maintain connections under stress, and trust that what can be built together proves stronger than what keeps us apart.

The psychological dimensions of bridge-building deserve deeper exploration, particularly the internal work required of individuals who choose to reach across divides in a polarized environment. Bridge-building is not only an institutional or structural challenge but also a profoundly personal one that demands emotional labor, cognitive flexibility, and moral courage. Those who maintain friendships or working relationships across political divides often report experiencing social pressure from their own tribes to sever these connections, to prove loyalty by rejecting the other side. This pressure can be subtle—the raised eyebrows when mentioning a friendship with someone of opposing views, the jokes that assume everyone present shares the same political perspective, the social media dynamics that reward tribal performance and punish nuance. Or it can be explicit—family members demanding that relatives choose between political allegiance and family ties, activist communities that practice "call-out culture" ostracizing members who engage respectfully with ideological opponents, workplace environments where expressing certain views or associations risks professional consequences. Sustaining bridging relationships in such contexts requires what might be called "bridge-keeper resilience"—the capacity to withstand social costs, to tolerate the discomfort of holding complexity in a culture that demands simplicity, and to maintain relationship commitments even when doing so brings no immediate reward and considerable immediate cost.

This personal dimension of bridge-building also involves developing specific psychological skills and practices that enable productive engagement across differences. The capacity for "perspective-taking"—genuinely imagining how situations appear from another person's vantage point—must be cultivated deliberately, as our default cognitive patterns favor confirming our existing beliefs and dismissing contrary views. "Emotional regulation" becomes essential when encountering views that trigger strong reactions, as bridging conversations collapse when participants cannot manage their own emotional responses sufficiently to remain engaged rather than attacking or withdrawing. "Charitable interpretation"—the practice of interpreting ambiguous statements in the most generous rather than the most damning way possible—counteracts the tendency toward "motive attribution asymmetry," in which we assume good intentions for our own side's actions while attributing malice to the other side. These skills do not come naturally to most people; they must be taught, modeled, and practiced. Educational programs focused on constructive dialogue, meditation, and contemplative practices that cultivate self-awareness and equanimity, and structured intergroup dialogue processes that scaffold difficult conversations, all represent approaches to developing these capacities at the individual level. Without sufficient numbers of people equipped with these skills, even well-designed institutional bridges will lack the human traffic necessary to make them meaningful.

The international dimensions of bridge-building offer both cautionary tales and inspiring examples that illuminate our own challenges. Societies recovering from violent conflict—Northern Ireland after the Troubles, Rwanda after the genocide, South Africa after apartheid—have confronted divisions far more extreme than those facing most contemporary democracies, yet their experiences with reconciliation processes yield valuable lessons. Truth and reconciliation commissions demonstrate that acknowledging past injuries rather than pretending they didn't occur can paradoxically enable moving forward. However, their success depends heavily on implementation details and broader institutional contexts. Power-sharing arrangements that guarantee representation for previously excluded groups can reduce zero-sum political competition, though they also risk entrenching the very divisions they aim to overcome. Integrated schools and housing in post-conflict societies show both the potential and the limitations of contact theory at the societal scale. These international examples remind us that bridge-building after deep division is possible but requires sustained commitment, institutional support, and willingness to address root causes rather than merely surface manifestations of conflict. They also highlight that successful bridging need not mean eliminating all differences or achieving complete consensus, but instead establishing sufficient trust and institutional frameworks that enable coexistence and cooperation despite ongoing disagreement over significant matters.

Chapter 5: The Power of Empathy

The reconstruction of fractured societies ultimately depends not merely on structural reforms, institutional innovations, or procedural dialogues, but on something far more fundamental and far more challenging to cultivate: the capacity to feel with and for those we perceive as different from ourselves. Empathy—that remarkable human ability to emotionally resonate with another's experience, to imaginatively inhabit their perspective, to feel their pain as though it were our own—represents both the foundation upon which all other reunification efforts must rest and the outcome toward which they all ultimately aim. Yet empathy in our current moment faces extraordinary challenges. The same technological and social forces that have fractured our shared tapestry have simultaneously eroded our empathic capacities, creating what might be termed an "empathy recession" that deepens just when we need this faculty most urgently. The psychological distance between groups has grown so vast that the imaginative leap required to feel with someone from the "other side genuinely can seem impossible, a bridge too far even for the most generous spirit. Understanding how empathy functions, why it has diminished, and how it might be restored represents crucial work for anyone committed to social reunification, for without empathy's animating force, all our dialogues become mere rituals, all our bridges become hollow structures that no one truly wishes to cross.

The neuroscience of empathy reveals something both encouraging and troubling about this capacity: it is simultaneously hardwired into our biology and remarkably susceptible to contextual factors that can amplify or suppress its expression. Mirror neurons fire in our brains when we observe others experiencing emotion, creating a literal neural resonance that forms the biological substrate of empathic response. This automatic, pre-cognitive reaction suggests that empathy is not simply a moral choice we make but an evolved capacity that helped our ancestors survive through cooperation and mutual care. Infants display rudimentary empathic responses within hours of birth, crying in response to the distress of other infants, suggesting this capacity predates language, culture, and conscious choice. Yet the very research that demonstrates empathy's biological basis also reveals its profound limitations and vulnerabilities. Empathy is most strongly activated toward those we perceive as similar to ourselves —part of our in-group, sharing our characteristics and identities. The same neural circuits that fire vigorously when we witness the suffering of someone we identify with can remain remarkably quiet when we observe identical suffering in someone we perceive as fundamentally different. Brain imaging studies have documented this disturbing reality. When participants view members of stigmatized out-groups experiencing pain, the regions associated with empathic response show significantly reduced activation compared to when they view in-group members in identical circumstances. This neural parochialism means that our empathic capacities, rather than naturally extending to all humanity, actually reinforce the very divisions we seek to overcome. The biological substrate that should unite us instead mirrors and amplifies our social fractures.

This selective empathy becomes particularly pronounced and problematic in conditions of intergroup conflict and perceived threat. When we feel our group is endangered and perceive those different from us as potential adversaries, our empathic responses undergo a kind of strategic retreat, withdrawing from those labeled as enemies or competitors. This narrowing serves a functional purpose from an evolutionary perspective—it concentrates our caring resources on those most likely to reciprocate, maintains group cohesion in the face of external challenges, and prevents exploitation by out-group members who might take advantage of our concern without offering reciprocal care. However, in complex modern societies where we must coexist with vast numbers of people different from ourselves, where our well-being depends on cooperation across group lines, and where the "enemies" we face are often fellow citizens with different political views rather than genuinely threatening adversaries, this empathic narrowing becomes profoundly maladaptive. It transforms manageable disagreements into moral chasms, converts political opponents into monsters who deserve our contempt rather than our understanding, and creates self-reinforcing cycles in which each group's empathic withdrawal from the other validates and intensifies the reciprocal withdrawal. The result is a kind of mutual empathetic disinvestment in which neither side truly tries to understand the other's experiences, fears, and aspirations, and each hardened attitude confirms the other's assumption that empathy would be wasted on such people.

The contemporary information environment has accelerated and intensified this empathic recession in ways that previous generations never had to confront. Social media platforms, through their algorithmic curation and structural incentives, systematically expose us to the most outrageous, offensive, and extreme statements from those we disagree with while filtering out the more moderate, nuanced, and sympathetic expressions that might generate empathic connection. We encounter the "other side" not through direct personal interaction with actual human beings but through carefully selected examples of their worst behavior, most inflammatory rhetoric, and least defensible positions. These digital caricatures become the basis for our understanding of entire groups, creating what might be termed "empathy-incompatible representations" that make genuine fellow-feeling nearly impossible. When your primary exposure to political conservatives consists of viral videos of their most extreme members saying things deliberately calculated to provoke outrage, or when your understanding of progressive activists comes entirely from screenshots of their most radical demands stripped of all context, the imaginative work required for empathy confronts an enormous obstacle. You are asked to empathize not with actual human beings in their full complexity but with algorithmically selected worst-case scenarios designed to trigger disgust and anger rather than understanding. The platforms profit from engagement, and nothing generates engagement quite like moral outrage directed at an out-group, so the incentive structures governing our information consumption actively work against the cultivation of empathy across difference.

The phenomenon of "empathic override" represents another significant challenge in divided societies. Even when individuals possess the capacity for empathy and genuinely wish to understand those different from themselves, competing cognitive and emotional processes can override these empathic impulses. Ideology serves as one powerful override mechanism. When we have firm ideological commitments to particular frameworks for understanding the world, empathic information that contradicts these frameworks often gets dismissed or rationalized away. Suppose your ideological system holds that poverty results primarily from individual choices and character flaws, empathic exposure to the genuine suffering of impoverished individuals, and the structural barriers they face, which creates uncomfortable cognitive dissonance. One response is to adjust your ideology to accommodate this empathic information. Still, an equally common response is to override the empathic impulse itself, finding reasons why this particular case is exceptional, why the suffering is exaggerated or self-inflicted, or why empathic concern would actually be counterproductive. Similarly, when empathy might lead us toward conclusions that threaten our group's interests or status, we often unconsciously suppress these empathic responses before they can influence our judgment. Research on racial empathy gaps, for instance, demonstrates that white Americans usually show reduced empathic responses to Black suffering when acknowledging that suffering would implicitly indict systems from which they benefit. This is not necessarily conscious racism but rather an unconscious protective mechanism that shields us from the guilt, responsibility, and potential loss of status that genuine empathy might demand. The result is a society where people are not exactly lacking in empathic capacity but have developed sophisticated mechanisms for selectively deactivating that capacity when it becomes inconvenient or threatening.

Yet despite these formidable obstacles, empathy retains a remarkable power to transform individual perspectives and, through the accumulation of such transformations, to reshape social relations. Numerous intervention studies have demonstrated that empathy can be cultivated, extended, and directed toward those we initially perceived as alien or unsympathetic. Personal narrative represents one of the most potent tools for this empathic expansion. When we encounter stories told in the first person by members of out-groups, describing their experiences, emotions, and the reasoning behind their choices in their own words rather than through the filter of media representation or political rhetoric, our empathic responses activate far more reliably than when we encounter those same groups through abstract argument or statistical data. A conservative Christian who has only encountered LGBTQ individuals through political debates about bathroom access or wedding cakes may possess a set of abstract opinions on these issues that feel principled but show no empathic engagement with actual queer lives. That same person, upon reading a detailed first-person account of a transgender teenager's experiences of dysphoria, family rejection, and eventual self-acceptance, often finds something shifting in their emotional landscape. They do not necessarily abandon their previous positions immediately, but the issue becomes populated with human beings deserving of concern rather than remaining purely abstract. This narrative-induced empathy does not guarantee agreement, but it fundamentally alters the terms of disagreement, making it less likely to take dehumanizing forms and more likely to acknowledge the genuine stakes involved for all parties.

The practice of "empathic inquiry" offers another powerful approach to expanding our capacity for feeling with those different from ourselves. Unlike the structured dialogue processes explored in earlier chapters, which focus on creating spaces for exchange and mutual understanding, empathic inquiry targets explicitly the cultivation of emotional resonance and imaginative identification. It involves deliberately seeking out opportunities to understand not just what others think but what they feel, not just their arguments but their fears and hopes, not just their positions but their lived experiences. This might take the form of reading memoirs from people across political divides, deliberately consuming media that presents sympathetic portraits of out-groups, or engaging in conversations where the explicit goal is understanding emotional reality rather than debating ideas. The psychologist Paul Bloom has distinguished between "cognitive empathy"—understanding what someone thinks and feels—and "emotional empathy"— actually sharing those feelings—and has controversially argued that the former might be more useful than the latter for ethical decision-making. However, in the specific context of social reunification, both forms prove essential. Cognitive empathy without emotional resonance can lead to strategic manipulation, understanding others only to oppose them more effectively. Emotional empathy without cognitive understanding can lead to selective, even counterproductive, caring. The integration of both—truly understanding another's situation and genuinely feeling concern for their wellbeing—creates the foundation for relationships that can survive disagreement and for societies that can maintain cohesion despite difference.

The concept of "empathic imagination" extends these capacities further by recognizing that empathy need not depend entirely on direct encounter or personal narrative. We can cultivate the ability to imaginatively reconstruct the experiences, constraints, and perspectives of those we have never met and may never meet. This requires what the philosopher Martha Nussbaum calls "narrative imagination"—the capacity to think what it might be like to be in the shoes of someone different from ourselves, to see how the world looks from that perspective, and to understand how various experiences and social positions shape not just opinions but entire ways of being in the world. Literature has long served this function, allowing readers to temporarily inhabit the consciousness of characters unlike themselves and thus expand the circle of those for whom they can feel genuine concern. The contemporary poet Naomi Shihab Nye captures this beautifully when she writes that empathy is "the only thing that can save us," but notes that it requires "stepping outside our own skins"—a radical act of imagination that our comfortable habits of mind naturally resist. In a reunification context, empathic imagination means actively working to understand not just individual perspectives but entire social positions—what it might be like to be a rural factory worker watching your community hollow out as manufacturing jobs disappear, what it might be like to be a young person of color navigating predominantly white institutions, what it might be like to be an evangelical Christian feeling that your values are being systematically marginalized in mainstream culture, what it might be like to be an immigrant navigating a new society while maintaining connection to your culture of origin. None of these imaginative exercises produces perfect understanding, and none substitutes for listening to actual members of these groups describe their own experiences. Still, they represent necessary preparation for that listening, creating mental frameworks that allow empathy to emerge when a genuine encounter occurs.

The relationship between empathy and justice requires careful consideration, particularly because empathy alone proves insufficient for social reunification and can sometimes actually obstruct justice. The philosopher Jesse Prinz has argued that empathy can be morally dangerous because it is partial, preferring the near over the far, the similar over the different, and the individual over the collective. He notes that we might feel tremendous empathy for an identified individual suffering before us while remaining unmoved by statistical information about thousands suffering at a distance, a phenomenon psychologists call "psychic numbing." This empathy bias means that our empathic responses might actually distort our moral judgments, leading us to allocate resources to those who generate the strongest empathic pull rather than to those who need help most urgently or where intervention would do the most good. Furthermore, empathy can be strategically deployed to manipulate us, with skilled communicators learning to trigger our empathic responses in ways that serve their interests rather than justice. Political campaigns routinely use individual suffering to generate empathic responses that support particular policies, even when those policies might not address the underlying problems or might create greater aggregate suffering. These legitimate concerns do not negate empathy's importance but suggest that it must be coupled with principles, systemic thinking, and commitment to justice that extends beyond empathic response. In the reunification context, this means using empathy as a motivating force and relationship foundation while simultaneously engaging in the more complex analytical work of understanding structural problems and identifying solutions that go beyond individual caring to institutional change.

The practice of "bidirectional empathy" addresses some of these limitations by recognizing that reunification requires not just one group empathizing with another but mutual empathy that flows in multiple directions simultaneously. In many divided societies, empathy conversations tend to be framed unidirectionally—privileged groups should develop empathy for marginalized groups, majority populations should empathize with minorities, and those benefiting from the status quo should feel for those harmed by it. These calls are valid and essential, but genuine reunification requires empathy to flow in all directions. Marginalized groups must develop empathy for the genuine fears and concerns of those in dominant positions, not because those fears necessarily justify existing arrangements, but because understanding them is necessary for finding pathways forward that address legitimate concerns rather than simply demanding surrender. Rural communities whose traditions and values have been casually dismissed by urban elites need empathy for their sense of being left behind, even as they are called to empathize with others experiencing their own forms of marginalization. Working-class voters who have supported populist movements need empathy for their economic anxieties and cultural dislocation, even as they are asked to extend empathy to immigrants and minorities. This bidirectional empathy does not imply moral equivalence between all positions or suggest that "both sides" are equally right or wrong. Instead, it recognizes that reunification requires understanding the full complexity of human motivation, acknowledging that people we disagree with rarely see themselves as villains but typically believe they are responding reasonably to genuine concerns, and creating space for all parties to feel that their experiences and fears have been taken seriously, even when their preferred solutions are not adopted.

The role of proximity in cultivating empathy cannot be overstated, despite the promises of our technologically mediated age to connect across distance. Genuine empathic bonds typically require sustained, personal interaction—not necessarily face-to-face, but certainly more substantial than the fleeting, curated encounters that characterize most social media interactions. The contact hypothesis in social psychology has long documented that prejudice tends to decrease and empathy tends to increase when members of different groups interact under conditions of equal status, common goals, and institutional support. Yet our contemporary society increasingly sorts itself into homogeneous clusters where such contact becomes rare. We live in ideologically uniform neighborhoods, work in politically homogeneous industries, socialize in echo chambers, and worship in congregations that share our values. This "big sort" means that many of us go through daily life rarely encountering, in any meaningful way, people who see the world fundamentally differently than we do. The resulting empathy deficit cannot be addressed through information alone—reading about people different from ourselves, however valuable, does not substitute for actually knowing them, working alongside them, facing shared challenges with them, and discovering their humanity through a sustained relationship. This reality underscores the crucial importance of integrated spaces—neighborhoods, schools, workplaces, community organizations, and civic institutions — where people from different backgrounds, identities, and perspectives necessarily interact and collaborate. Such integration often faces fierce resistance because homogeneity is comfortable. Still, the empathic gains from genuine integration justify the discomfort, creating relationships that can survive the political divisions that might otherwise completely separate us.

The transformation from empathy to solidarity represents a crucial progression in the reunification process, yet one that frequently stalls because we misunderstand the relationship between these concepts. Empathy means feeling with someone —empathizing with their experience —but it often remains passive—a feeling we have without necessarily acting on it. Solidarity takes empathy's emotional insight and converts it into committed action, standing alongside others in their struggles even when those struggles are not our own and even at cost to ourselves. The journey from empathy to solidarity requires moving beyond the question "How would I feel in their situation?" to the question "What am I called to do given their situation?" and ultimately to "How can I align myself with their efforts to improve their situation?" This transformation proves difficult precisely because solidarity demands more than empathy. It requires sustained commitment rather than momentary feeling, practical sacrifice rather than emotional recognition, and willingness to accept leadership from those whose experiences we are trying to support rather than assuming our empathic insight gives us authority to speak for them. The most powerful movements for social reunification typically combine the emotional force of empathy with the practical commitment of solidarity, creating coalitions in which members genuinely care for one another's well-being and actively work to address each other's concerns. The civil rights movement at its best exemplified this combination, with Black organizers leading the struggle. At the same time, white allies contributed their specific resources and took genuine risks, motivated by empathy but manifesting solidarity through action. The contemporary challenge is to cultivate such transformative empathy-to-solidarity pathways across our current divides, creating commitments that survive the inevitable tensions and setbacks inherent in reunification work.

The practice of "empathic accountability" offers a framework for addressing the tension between empathic understanding and the need to change certain behaviors and attitudes. One persistent criticism of empathy in political contexts is that it can enable harmful behavior by providing endless knowledge for those who cause harm rather than demanding accountability and change. If we are infinitely empathic toward those who express racist views, understanding the fears and cultural contexts that produced those views, when do we insist that such views are unacceptable regardless of their origins? If we empathize with those who have benefited from unjust systems, understanding how difficult it is to acknowledge privilege and how threatening systemic change feels, does that empathy become an excuse for allowing unjust systems to persist? Empathic accountability navigates this tension by combining a genuine understanding of how people came to hold problematic positions or engage in harmful behaviors with clear expectations that they take responsibility for impact and commit to change. It means saying, "I understand the circumstances and experiences that shaped your views, and I recognize that from your position, they may have seemed reasonable, but the impact of these views causes real harm to real people, and I need you to grapple with that harm and change your behavior." This approach proves far more effective than shame-based accountability, which often produces defensiveness and retrenchment, because it provides a pathway to change that does not require people to see themselves as fundamentally flawed. Research on transformative justice demonstrates that people are most capable of genuine change when they feel understood and respected, even as their actions are challenged, when accountability is delivered within a context of continued relationship rather than exile from moral community. Empathic accountability thus becomes a reunification tool rather than an obstacle to it, allowing society to maintain standards and insist on change while also providing pathways back to the community for those willing to do the necessary work.

The cultivation of empathy at scale—moving beyond individual empathic capacity to creating empathic cultures and institutions—represents the ultimate challenge for societies seeking reunification. Individual empathy remains fragile and easily overwhelmed by situational factors, ideology, and intergroup dynamics. For empathy to truly reshape social relations, it must become embedded in our institutional practices, cultural norms, and educational systems. What would an empathic education system look like? One that teaches history from multiple perspectives, including those of groups that have been marginalized; that includes literature and arts representing diverse experiences; that creates opportunities for students from different backgrounds to collaborate on meaningful projects; that explicitly teaches empathic skills and emotional intelligence rather than assuming these capacities develop automatically; and that models empathic responses to conflict in its own disciplinary and pedagogical practices. What would empathic institutions look like? Organizations that build empathic consideration into their decision-making processes, regularly asking not just "What does the data suggest?" but "How will different stakeholders experience this decision?"; that create mechanisms for those affected by decisions to have meaningful input; that train leaders in empathic listening and perspective-taking; and that reward rather than punish empathic attention to complexity and human impact. What would an empathic political culture look like? One that demands more from leaders than skillful articulation of in-group grievances, that rewards genuine understanding of diverse constituents rather than pure partisan loyalty, that creates spaces for vulnerable truth-telling rather than only strategic positioning, and that allows public figures to acknowledge the legitimate concerns of those they ultimately disagree with without this acknowledgment being weaponized as weakness or betrayal. These systemic and cultural manifestations of empathy do not arise spontaneously. Still, they must be deliberately cultivated through sustained effort, institutional reform, and continuous modeling of empathic practices, even when they feel costly or inefficient in the moment.

The power of empathy to reunify fractured societies ultimately rests not in its ability to eliminate disagreement or produce consensus on contested issues, but in its capacity to preserve our mutual recognition of shared humanity even across profound differences. Empathy does not require us to approve of all behaviors, accept all perspectives as equally valid, or abandon our own commitments and principles. It does not mean that all divisions can be bridged through better understanding or that genuine conflicts of interest disappear when we feel for those on the other side. What empathy offers is something both more modest and more profound: the possibility of remaining in relationship with those we disagree with, of seeing opponents as mistaken human beings rather than monsters beyond the moral community, of maintaining the social bonds that allow democratic contestation to remain within peaceful bounds, and of preserving the possibility that today's adversaries might become tomorrow's collaborators when circumstances shift and new issues emerge. In societies that have successfully navigated deep divisions without collapsing into violence or permanent rupture, empathy has served as the glue holding the social fabric together even when every thread seemed to pull in different directions. It reminds us that the person across the divide shares our fundamental humanity, experiences joy and suffering much as we do, loves their children and hopes for their future with the same intensity we feel, and deserves the basic respect that this recognition demands. This empathic foundation allows all the other reunification work—dialogue, bridge-building, institutional reform, and political negotiation—to proceed on ground that remains firm enough to support the weight of our differences. Without empathy, these processes become mechanical exercises unlikely to produce lasting reconciliation. With empathy, they become animated by genuine care for our collective future, creating the possibility not merely of peaceful coexistence but of an authentic community that honors both our connections and our differences.

Chapter 6: Stories of Reconciliation

The abstract principles of dialogue, bridge-building, and empathy find their most compelling expression not in theoretical frameworks but in the lived experiences of human beings who have traversed the rugged terrain from enmity to understanding. While we have explored the mechanisms and processes through which societies can heal their divisions, the actual test of these concepts lies in their embodiment by real people facing actual conflicts. The stories that follow are not fairy tales of effortless harmony or sanitized narratives that minimize the pain of division, but rather honest accounts of the messy, uncertain, and profoundly transformative work of reconciliation as it unfolds in specific contexts with particular individuals. These narratives reveal patterns that transcend their immediate circumstances, offering insights into the universal dynamics of human reconnection while remaining firmly grounded in the specific details that make each story of reconciliation unique and irreplaceable.

Consider the remarkable transformation that occurred in a small textile town in the American South, where generations of economic decline had created fault lines that seemed to divide the community into irreconcilable camps. The closure of the main factory had not affected all residents equally—some had savings and education to cushion their transition, while others faced immediate destitution. This economic stratification aligned uncomfortably with existing racial divisions, creating a toxic situation where every conversation about the town's future became a referendum on historical injustices and present grievances. The downtown area became a contested space where different groups advanced opposing narratives about what had happened and who was to blame, with some residents insisting that changing economic forces were beyond anyone's control. In contrast, others pointed to specific decisions by specific people that had betrayed the community's working families. Into this environment stepped Maria Chen, a woman who had left the town thirty years earlier for college and a career in urban planning, returning to care for her aging parents and finding a community she barely recognized in its depth of mutual suspicion and resentment.

Maria's contribution to her hometown's healing began not with any grand plan but with a simple observation during a contentious town hall meeting about redevelopment proposals. She noticed that people who had been neighbors for decades no longer knew basic facts about each other's lives—who had lost jobs, who was struggling with medical bills, who was caring for elderly parents while working multiple part-time positions. The community had become so fragmented that its members had stopped seeing each other as fully human, instead reducing neighbors to representatives of political positions or demographic categories. Her insight was that before any substantive policy discussions could occur productively, people needed to reestablish a basic understanding of each other's actual circumstances rather than rely on assumptions filtered through ideological lenses. She began organizing what she called "porch conversations"—small gatherings of four to six people from different backgrounds who would meet on someone's front porch or in their living room for no other purpose than to share their personal stories from the past 10 years. The rules were deliberately minimal: speak from your own experience, listen without interrupting, and ask questions only to understand better, not to challenge or debate.

The first few months of these gatherings produced little noticeable progress toward resolving the town's deep divisions. People shared stories that confirmed their existing grievances, sometimes breaking down as they recounted losses and betrayals. Several participants dropped out, claiming the conversations were pointless emotional exercises that avoided the real political and economic decisions the town needed to make. Yet Maria persisted, and something subtle began to shift among those who continued to participate. A white small business owner who had initially blamed "government handouts" for creating "dependency" found himself weeping as he heard a Black single mother describe her daughter's struggles with diabetes and the impossible choices she faced between paying for insulin and keeping their electricity on. A progressive activist who had dismissed working-class white residents as irredeemably racist heard a laid-off factory worker describe watching his wife succumb to opioid addiction after a workplace injury, realizing with shock that this man's lived experience of systemic abandonment paralleled narratives she had previously reserved for urban communities of color. These were not moments of complete transformation where lifelong beliefs instantly evaporated, but rather the beginning of complications in previously simple narratives, the introduction of contradictions that made blanket judgments harder to sustain.

What emerged from these porch conversations over eighteen months was not consensus about policy solutions or agreement about historical responsibility, but something more fundamental: a restored recognition of shared humanity and interconnected fate. Participants still disagreed about taxation levels, social programs, and economic development strategies. Still, they could no longer maintain the psychological distance that had made these disagreements into existential conflicts between wholly different kinds of people with incompatible values. The business owner who had wept for the diabetic child found himself quietly providing job flexibility for the mother, even though his political views about government programs had not dramatically shifted. The progressive activist began including working-class white voices in her advocacy work, recognizing that economic justice was not a zero-sum competition among demographic groups but a shared challenge that required coalition. When the town eventually developed a compromise redevelopment plan that included both business incentives and social support mechanisms, it succeeded not because everyone had converted to a common ideology, but because enough people had undergone a process that restored their capacity to see neighbors as neighbors rather than enemies in a culture war.

The story from that Southern textile town illustrates a pattern visible in reconciliation processes around the world: the critical importance of creating spaces where people encounter each other's actual humanity before attempting to resolve substantive disagreements. This sequence—human recognition before political resolution—reverses the approach often attempted in deeply divided communities, where leaders assume that if they can find the right policy compromise, relationships will naturally improve. Yet reconciliation rarely proceeds so logically. The policies that prove durable are those built on a foundation of restored relationships, where participants view the agreement not as a temporary truce between enemies but as a mutual commitment among people who have come to care about each other's well-being despite their differences. This does not mean that relationship-building alone solves everything—the textile town still faced enormous economic challenges and continuing racial tensions—but it creates the social infrastructure necessary for working through complex problems without fragmenting into separate camps that cannot collaborate.

Halfway around the world, a different story of reconciliation unfolded in a divided village in Rwanda's eastern hills, where the 1994 genocide had left wounds that seemed impossible to heal. In this community, perpetrators and survivors lived side by side, the terrible intimacy of knowing exactly who had killed whose family members creating a daily torture of proximity. The official government-sponsored reconciliation processes had established formal mechanisms for confession, forgiveness, and reintegration. Still, in this particular village, these structures had produced only surface compliance rather than genuine reconciliation. Jean-Baptiste Habimana, who had lost most of his family in the violence, found himself consumed by hatred for his neighbor Alphonse Nkurunziza, who had participated in the killings and served time in prison before returning to the village. The two men would pass each other on the path to the well without acknowledgment, each carrying the weight of history that made ordinary neighborliness impossible. Jean-Baptiste attended church services where he mechanically recited words about forgiveness while nurturing fantasies of revenge, knowing that his bitterness was destroying him, but unable to relinquish it without feeling he was betraying his murdered family.

The breakthrough in this impossible situation came not from either man but from their children. Jean-Baptiste's eight-year-old daughter Aline and Alphonse's son Emmanuel attended the same school and had become friends before learning of their fathers' connection to the genocide. When the children discovered the history that supposedly made their friendship impossible, they refused to accept that the sins of the fathers must define their own relationship. Their innocent defiance of inherited enmity forced both men to confront questions they had avoided: What exactly would they be teaching their children if they insisted on perpetual hatred? Could genuine love for their children coexist with an absolute refusal to see any humanity in the other's child, who would suffer if their friendship were forbidden? The children became, in effect, ambassadors across an impossible divide, carrying between the households small communications that neither man could have initiated himself. Emmanuel brought his father's apology to Jean-Baptiste's door, not the formal apology required by legal processes but a personal acknowledgment that what he had done to Jean-Baptiste's family was unforgivable and that he understood if Jean-Baptiste could never move beyond hatred. This unexpected humility, conveyed through the voice of an innocent child, broke something in Jean-Baptiste's calcified grief.

What followed was not instant reconciliation but a painstaking process of rebuilding minimal trust between two men who would never be friends, yet who discovered they could become something more complex: neighbors who had caused each other irreparable harm, yet chose to build a future that did not require their children to inherit their trauma. Jean-Baptiste never declared that he forgave Alphonse in any complete sense—how could anyone forgive the murder of their family?—but he made a different choice: to cease actively cultivating his hatred, to acknowledge Alphonse's humanity without excusing his actions, and to participate in small cooperative activities that the community needed to function. They worked together on a community irrigation project, their shared labor creating a practical foundation that preceded any emotional resolution. They attended village meetings where both contributed to decisions about the community's future, discovering that they could sometimes agree about what the village needed even though this agreement did not erase the past. Most significantly, they modeled for their children and the watching community that coexistence after atrocity was possible without pretending the atrocity had not occurred or that it had been less terrible than it was.

The Rwandan story reveals dimensions of reconciliation that challenge simplistic notions of what healing must look like. Jean-Baptiste did not have to declare that he fully forgave Alphonse, nor did he have to claim that his heart had been entirely emptied of anger. The reconciliation that emerged was not a triumphant transcendence of the past but a hard-won agreement to live differently with permanent scars. This more modest but perhaps more sustainable form of reconciliation acknowledges that some harms are too deep for complete healing in any conventional sense, yet insists that even the most profound damage need not dictate every subsequent interaction. The key was finding practical domains of cooperation that created new experiences alongside the terrible memories, gradually adding complexity to a relationship defined entirely by one catastrophic period. The irrigation project, the school meetings, the agricultural cooperative—these mundane activities created alternative content for the relationship between the two men, not replacing the genocide memory but adding other layers that made it possible to interact without every encounter being a re-traumatization.

A third story of reconciliation emerges from a suburban American community torn apart not by economic collapse or historical atrocity but by the divisive politics of the contemporary moment. In this affluent neighborhood of educated professionals, political polarization had transformed longtime friends into strangers who crossed the street to avoid each other. The 2016 election and its aftermath created a social environment in which yard signs became declarations of tribal loyalty and social media posts served as litmus tests for continued relationships. Two women who had been close friends for fifteen years—sharing carpools, celebrating children's birthdays together, supporting each other through divorces and job losses—found their friendship disintegrating as their political views diverged. Sarah Matthews, who became increasingly progressive in her politics, found herself unable to understand how her friend Rebecca Sullivan could support politicians and policies that Sarah viewed as existentially threatening to vulnerable populations. Rebecca, who moved in a more conservative direction, felt judged and dismissed by Sarah's increasingly strident social media posts that seemed to paint anyone who disagreed as morally deficient. Their text message exchanges became tense and sparse, then stopped altogether, each woman nursing hurt and anger about the other's perceived betrayal.

The rupture between Sarah and Rebecca might have become permanent — another casualty of the forces pulling society apart — except for an unexpected catalyst. Rebecca's teenage son attempted suicide after severe bullying at school, and when Sarah heard the news, something cut through all the political animosity. She showed up at the hospital not with any agenda or expectation of reconciliation but simply because a child she had watched grow up was suffering, and a friend she had once loved was in crisis. The hours they spent together in that hospital waiting room created a temporary suspension of their political conflict, a space where their shared humanity as mothers and as people who had once deeply cared for each other became more immediate than their disagreements about immigration policy or healthcare reform. They did not resolve their political differences in that hospital, nor did they pretend those differences did not matter. Still, they rediscovered a dimension of their relationship that transcended political categories—a genuine concern for each other's well-being that their ideological conflict had obscured but not destroyed.

The rebuilding of Sarah and Rebecca's friendship progressed slowly and remained marked by tension. They agreed explicitly that they would not try to convert each other politically. Still, they would instead focus on the aspects of their lives and values that remained shared despite their political divergence. This was not an avoidance of complex topics but a recognition that their friendship had become nothing but complex issues, leaving no room for the other dimensions that had initially drawn them together. They resumed their habit of walking together several mornings a week, during which they talked about their children, their aging parents, their work frustrations, and their personal struggles with meaning and purpose in middle age. Political subjects arose naturally in these conversations, but within a relational context that prevented any single disagreement from becoming a relationship-ending crisis. Sarah began to understand that Rebecca's political views were rooted in genuine concerns about cultural change, economic uncertainty, and a sense of being dismissed by coastal elites, even though Sarah still disagreed with Rebecca's conclusions about appropriate policy responses. Rebecca recognized that Sarah's progressive activism emerged from real encounters with injustice and from a moral framework that valued inclusion and protection of vulnerable people, even though Rebecca worried about the practical consequences of some policies Sarah supported.

What makes the story of Sarah and Rebecca particularly instructive is that it illustrates reconciliation in an environment where the stakes might seem lower than genocide or economic devastation, yet where the psychological dynamics are experienced by millions of people in contemporary societies. The political divisions that shattered their friendship are tearing apart families, neighborhoods, congregations, and civic organizations throughout developed democracies. Their path back to relationship models a form of reconciliation appropriate to this context: not agreement about the fundamental political questions dividing society, but a commitment to maintaining the relationship despite those disagreements, based on recognition that political positions do not capture the full complexity of any human being. They discovered that they could vote differently, advocate for opposing policies, and even argue passionately about political issues while still being friends who showed up for each other's family crises, celebrated each other's achievements, and maintained the bonds that connected their lives. This form of reconciliation does not resolve the political conflicts fragmenting society. Still, it prevents those conflicts from achieving total victory by preserving cross-cutting ties that create incentives for continued communication and reduced demonization.

These three stories—from the American South, from Rwanda, and from suburban America—reveal common patterns in the process of reconciliation despite their vastly different contexts and scales of conflict. In each case, reconciliation required a catalyst that disrupted the existing pattern of avoidance or hostility, creating an opening for a different interaction. Maria Chen's porch conversations, the innocent friendship between Jean-Baptiste's and Alphonse's children, and Rebecca's son's crisis all functioned as interruptions to established patterns, moments when the ordinary defenses and distancing mechanisms were temporarily lowered. These catalysts did not guarantee reconciliation—many similar openings fail to produce transformation—but they created conditions where reconciliation became possible by forcing people out of their established roles and into more complex human encounters. The catalysts worked not by solving the substantive problems that divided people but by creating experiences that complicated simple narratives of blame and opposition.

Additionally, each story illustrates that reconciliation proceeds not through abstract declarations but through specific, often modest actions that create new experiences alongside terrible memories or bitter conflicts. The irrigation project in Rwanda, the porch conversations in the textile town, and the morning walks between Sarah and Rebecca all provided concrete activities that gave people something to do together beyond negotiating their disagreements. This practical dimension of reconciliation is crucial because it creates positive content in relationships that had been defined entirely by conflict. The shared activities need not be profound or overtly related to the source of division; indeed, their very ordinariness can be therapeutic, establishing that people who disagree about important matters can still collaborate on ordinary tasks. These mundane cooperations gradually rebuild the muscle memory of working together, creating experiences that can be drawn upon when conflicts inevitably arise again.

Furthermore, all three stories demonstrate that sustainable reconciliation does not require complete forgiveness, thorough agreement, or total transformation of the people involved. Jean-Baptiste never claimed to have fully forgiven Alphonse; the textile town's residents continued to disagree over many policy questions, and Sarah and Rebecca maintained divergent political views. Yet reconciliation occurred nonetheless, taking forms appropriate to each situation. This more modest understanding of what reconciliation means is crucial for scaling these insights to larger social conflicts. If reconciliation required every victim to achieve complete forgiveness of every perpetrator, every political opponent to convert to their rival's worldview, or every hurt to be fully healed, then reconciliation in deeply divided societies would be impossible. Instead, these stories suggest that reconciliation can mean establishing sufficient trust and goodwill to enable coexistence and cooperation despite continuing disagreements, unresolved pain, and incomplete healing. This is not a failure of reconciliation but rather a realistic recognition of what is possible for human beings dealing with genuine harm, profound difference, and limited emotional capacity.

The stories also reveal the crucial role of time in reconciliation processes. None of these transformations occurred quickly, and attempts to rush reconciliation in any of the situations would likely have failed or produced only superficial compliance. Maria's porch conversations continued for eighteen months before producing visible changes in the town's dynamics. Jean-Baptiste and Alphonse worked together on practical projects for years before developing even the modest relationship they achieved. Setbacks and ongoing tensions marked Sarah and Rebecca's reconciliation over several years. This temporal dimension of reconciliation challenges the impatience of contemporary culture, which prefers instant solutions and dramatic transformations. Yet genuine reconciliation after deep division requires time for new experiences to accumulate, for trust to develop incrementally, and for the power of terrible memories to gradually diminish without being erased. The work cannot be rushed because it involves changing deeply ingrained emotional patterns, learned responses to threat, and identity commitments that have become central to how people understand themselves. The passage of time itself does not heal divisions, but time during which new experiences occur and different patterns are practiced is essential for reconciliation to go beyond the superficial.

Another pattern visible across these stories is the importance of third parties who facilitate reconciliation without being directly invested in the particular conflict. Maria Chen could play her role precisely because she had been away from the town during its worst conflicts, bringing an outsider's perspective combined with an insider's love for the community. The children in Rwanda bridged a divide their fathers could not cross themselves, their innocence providing a space that was not burdened by direct participation in the genocide. Even in Sarah and Rebecca's story, the son whose crisis catalyzed their reconciliation was separate from their political conflict, his suffering creating a domain where their differences became temporarily irrelevant. These third-party presences suggest that reconciliation often requires spaces or relationships that are not themselves corrupted by the conflict, sources of connection that can remind antagonists of something they share beyond their opposition. In designing interventions to promote reconciliation, creating and protecting such third-party spaces—whether they are children, shared community projects, or neutral facilitators—deserves particular attention.

The stories further illustrate that reconciliation is not a once-and-for-all achievement but an ongoing practice that must be maintained against continuing pressures toward division. The textile town faces regular new conflicts that test the relationships rebuilt through Maria's initiative. Jean-Baptiste and Alphonse must continually choose coexistence over the easier path of returned hatred. Sarah and Rebecca navigate continuing political crises that strain their recovered friendship. This understanding of reconciliation as practice rather than achievement is crucial for sustaining the work over time. If people believe that reconciliation means permanently solving the problem of division, they will be discouraged when conflicts inevitably resurface. But suppose reconciliation is understood as a commitment to working through conflicts without severing the relationship, to repeatedly choosing connection despite disagreement. In that case, the reappearance of tension is not failure but an expected challenge to be navigated using skills developed through previous reconciliation work.

Finally, these stories all demonstrate how individual reconciliation and systemic change interact in complex ways. Maria's porch conversations eventually influenced town policy through the relationships they rebuilt, though changing relationships was not originally a policy intervention. Jean-Baptiste and Alphonse's reconciliation occurred within Rwanda's national reconciliation process, but their personal journey went beyond what official mechanisms required or could guarantee. Sarah and Rebecca's recovered friendship did not change the political system that had poisoned their relationship. Yet, their example influenced their respective social networks, demonstrating to others that cross-political friendships remained possible. This suggests that reunifying divided societies requires both personal reconciliation and institutional change, neither of which is sufficient on its own. The structural reforms discussed in previous chapters create conditions that make reconciliation more likely, but they cannot guarantee that individuals will do the difficult personal work required. Conversely, individual reconciliations, even when numerous, cannot overcome structural incentives that reward division unless they eventually influence institutional arrangements. The most effective strategies for social reunification attend to both levels, recognizing that personal reconciliation and systemic change reinforce each other when pursued together.

These stories of reconciliation offer grounds for hope without minimizing the genuine difficulty of the work they represent. They demonstrate that even profound divisions can be crossed, not easily or completely, but sufficiently to enable shared life and collaborative work. They reveal patterns that apply across wildly different contexts, suggesting that insights about reconciliation can transfer from one situation to another despite different particulars. Yet they also insist on the irreducible particularity of each reconciliation story, how specific personalities, cultural contexts, and historical moments shape what is possible and which approaches might work. The art of applying these lessons involves holding both the universal patterns and the particular details in creative tension, neither assuming that what worked in one place will automatically transfer to another nor believing that every situation is so unique that no lessons can travel. As we consider how to reunify fractured societies at scale, these stories remind us that all reconciliation ultimately happens between particular human beings in specific moments, even as the structural conditions either facilitate or obstruct such encounters. The work ahead requires both creating systems that make reconciliation more likely and honoring the irreducible human dimensions that no system can fully script or guarantee.

Chapter 7: The Architecture of Trust

Suppose empathy provides the emotional foundation for reunification and stories illuminate the human dimensions of reconciliation. In that case, trust constitutes the essential architecture that determines whether fractured societies can actually function across their divisions. Trust is not merely a feeling or an attitude but a complex structural phenomenon—a form of social infrastructure as real and as necessary as bridges, roads, or communication networks. Without examining how trust is built, maintained, eroded, and reconstructed at both interpersonal and systemic levels, we cannot fully understand what reunification requires or why it so often fails despite good intentions. The architecture of trust encompasses the visible institutions that mediate our interactions and the invisible assumptions that allow us to predict others' behavior with sufficient confidence to cooperate despite uncertainty.

The metaphor of architecture proves particularly apt because trust, like physical architecture, involves load-bearing structures that enable certain activities while constraining others, visible surfaces that shape perception and interaction, and hidden foundations that determine whether the entire edifice will hold under stress. Architectural thinking requires us to consider not just individual components but how they fit together into functional systems, not just aesthetic appearance but structural integrity, not just current uses but future adaptability. When we speak of rebuilding trust in divided societies, we are fundamentally discussing architectural challenges: how to construct social systems that can bear the weight of continued disagreement, how to design institutions whose operations reinforce rather than undermine confidence in fairness and reciprocity, and how to create foundations strong enough to support reconciliation without requiring prior uniformity of belief or interest.

The fundamental challenge in trust architecture becomes immediately apparent when we recognize that trust operates simultaneously at multiple levels, each with different requirements and dynamics. Interpersonal trust between individuals develops through repeated interactions, demonstrated reliability, vulnerability shared and honored, and the gradual building of mutual understanding through direct experience. This form of trust is rich, textured, and deeply personal, but it cannot scale to encompass the millions of anonymous interactions that characterize modern societies. We cannot personally know everyone whose cooperation we require, cannot verify through direct experience the reliability of every institution on which we depend, and cannot maintain the kind of intimate knowledge that grounds interpersonal trust across vast and diverse populations. This creates the necessity for a different form of trust—systemic trust in institutions, processes, and abstract others who occupy social roles rather than personal relationships.

Systemic trust rests not on personal knowledge but on confidence in predictable patterns, institutional guarantees, professional standards, legal frameworks, and reputation systems that provide surrogates for direct experience. When you board an airplane, you trust not because you personally know the pilot, mechanics, and air traffic controllers, but because you have confidence in training systems, regulatory oversight, certification processes, and professional cultures that make competence and responsibility predictable. This form of trust enables the complex coordination required by modern societies, but it is also fundamentally fragile because it depends on institutions maintaining their integrity and effectiveness. When institutional performance erodes, when regulatory capture allows self-interested behavior to escape consequences, when professional standards fail to ensure competence or ethical conduct, systemic trust collapses rapidly and proves extraordinarily difficult to rebuild. In fractured societies, we often find that interpersonal trust may still exist within groups. In contrast, systemic trust in shared institutions has evaporated, creating situations where people can cooperate intensively with those they know personally while viewing broader society as fundamentally hostile or unreliable.

The erosion of systemic trust follows predictable patterns that have become painfully familiar across many contemporary societies. It typically begins with institutional failures that violate expectations—financial systems that reward recklessness while imposing costs on responsible actors, law enforcement agencies that apply force unevenly across different communities, political institutions that systematically favor connected interests over ordinary citizens, media organizations that prioritize engagement over accuracy, expert communities that fail to acknowledge uncertainty or error. Each violation chips away at the reservoir of trust that had accumulated through previous positive experiences, and critically, negative experiences carry far more weight than positive ones in shaping trust judgments. Research consistently demonstrates that trust builds slowly through many successful interactions but can collapse rapidly through a few dramatic violations. This asymmetry means that even relatively rare institutional failures can overwhelm many routine successes in shaping public confidence.

The collapse of systemic trust creates vicious cycles that accelerate fragmentation and make reunification progressively more difficult. When people lose confidence in shared institutions, they retreat into narrower circles of particularistic trust—family, immediate community, ethnic or religious group, ideological faction—where relationships can still be verified through direct experience or strong social bonds. This retreat, while psychologically understandable, further weakens the institutions that would need to function effectively to rebuild broader trust, creating a self-fulfilling prophecy. Institutions depend on public cooperation and compliance to function effectively; when citizens assume institutions are corrupt or incompetent, they withdraw their cooperation, which makes institutions less effective and further erodes trust. Similarly, when different groups abandon shared institutions in favor of parallel structures that serve only their own members, the common institutions lose the diverse participation necessary to maintain legitimacy across divisions, accelerating their transformation into instruments of particular factions rather than genuine public goods.

Understanding these dynamics reveals why superficial approaches to rebuilding trust inevitably fail and why reunification requires architectural thinking rather than merely public relations campaigns or appeals to goodwill. Public officials often respond to trust deficits by improving communication, rebranding institutions, or emphasizing positive stories while avoiding difficult accountability measures. These approaches typically backfire because they treat trust erosion as primarily a perception problem rather than a structural reality. When institutions have genuinely failed to perform their functions fairly or effectively, no amount of messaging can substitute for actual reform. Indeed, communication campaigns that emphasize trustworthiness without addressing underlying problems often accelerate trust collapse by demonstrating that officials either do not understand or do not care about the legitimate grievances driving public skepticism. Trust cannot be demanded or marketed; it must be earned through demonstrated competence, fairness, transparency, and accountability sustained over time.

The architectural approach to rebuilding trust begins not with communications strategies but with structural reforms that change how institutions actually function and how their performance can be verified. This requires what we might call "trust infrastructure"—systems explicitly designed to make institutional behavior more transparent, accountable, predictable, and aligned with public purposes rather than self-interested manipulation. Such infrastructure operates at multiple levels simultaneously. At the most basic level, it includes transparency mechanisms that allow outside observers to verify institutional performance rather than merely accepting official claims. Freedom of information systems, public meeting requirements, financial disclosure rules, data publication mandates, and whistleblower protections all serve to create visibility into otherwise opaque operations, allowing external verification of whether institutions are actually doing what they claim.

Beyond transparency, trust infrastructure requires accountability mechanisms that ensure institutional actors face meaningful consequences when they violate standards or fail to perform their responsibilities. The absence of accountability represents perhaps the most corrosive force undermining systemic trust in contemporary societies, as repeated examples demonstrate that powerful actors can engage in serious misconduct without facing consequences comparable to those imposed on ordinary citizens for far lesser transgressions. Financial executives whose recklessness triggered economic collapse are receiving government bailouts. At the same time, homeowners face foreclosure, and police officers who use excessive force remain on duty. In contrast, their victims face prosecution for minor infractions, while political officials caught in corruption stay in office, while low-level government employees lose their positions for minor violations. These patterns communicate unmistakably that institutions operate by different rules for different classes of people, destroying confidence that they serve public purposes rather than factional interests. Rebuilding trust requires not just stronger formal accountability systems but their consistent application across all actors, regardless of wealth, status, or political connection.

The architecture of accountability proves more complex than simply imposing punishments for misconduct, however, because overly rigid accountability systems can themselves undermine institutional effectiveness and public trust. When accountability mechanisms focus exclusively on compliance with narrow rules while ignoring substantive outcomes, they incentivize box-checking behavior that technically satisfies requirements while failing to serve genuine public purposes. When sanctions are so severe that they tolerate no error or uncertainty, institutions become paralyzed and risk-averse, unable to innovate or adapt to changing circumstances. When accountability processes lack procedural fairness or due process protections, they become tools of factional warfare rather than genuine quality control. Effective accountability architecture, therefore, requires careful calibration: clear standards for expected performance, genuine consequences for violations, but also recognition of the uncertainty inherent in complex systems, procedural fairness that protects against arbitrary punishment, and mechanisms that distinguish between good-faith errors made under challenging circumstances and genuine negligence or malfeasance.

A third essential component of trust infrastructure involves what might be termed "bridging institutions"— organizations and processes explicitly designed to function across group boundaries and maintain legitimacy with diverse constituencies simultaneously. In societies where trust has collapsed along identity lines, with different communities doubting that shared institutions serve their interests fairly, bridging institutions take on special importance as spaces where cross-cutting cooperation remains possible. These institutions succeed by maintaining genuine independence from factional capture, demonstrating competence in fulfilling their core functions despite political pressures, incorporating diverse perspectives into their decision-making, and being transparently committed to procedural fairness even when their decisions disappoint particular groups. The judiciary often serves this function when it maintains sufficient independence and procedural integrity to be seen as fair, even by parties who lose cases; certain professional bodies and scientific institutions can serve similar functions when they maintain a genuine commitment to evidence-based decision-making rather than political convenience; and some civic organizations become trusted bridging institutions through consistent commitment to their missions across political shifts.

The most successful bridging institutions share several architectural features that enable them to maintain cross-cutting legitimacy despite operating in fractured environments. First, they separate process from outcome in ways that allow multiple stakeholders to recognize decision-making as fair, even when they disagree with specific results. A judicial system maintains this quality when parties who lose cases can nonetheless acknowledge that procedures were followed correctly, evidence was considered reasonably, and rulings reflected legal standards rather than bias. Second, effective bridging institutions maintain transparent operations that allow external verification of their integrity while protecting enough operational independence to resist factional pressure. Third, they cultivate institutional cultures that value professional competence and ethical conduct over political alignment, creating organizations where individuals advance based on mastery of institutional purposes rather than loyalty to external factions. Fourth, they build reputational capital that provides some insulation from immediate political pressures, allowing them to make unpopular decisions when necessary without facing existential threats.

The challenge of constructing and maintaining bridging institutions in highly polarized environments cannot be overstated, particularly because their success makes them valuable targets for factional capture. Groups that control other institutions often seek to extend that control to bridging institutions as well, seeing their independence as an obstacle to be overcome rather than a public good to be protected. This creates what political scientists call "constitutional hardball"—attempts to manipulate institutional rules to achieve partisan advantage even though such manipulation undermines the long-term legitimacy and effectiveness of institutions. Court-packing schemes, partisan manipulation of supposedly independent regulatory agencies, political interference in professional military decision-making, ideological litmus tests for scientific advisory positions—these represent attempts to convert bridging institutions into instruments of factional interest, trading long-term institutional legitimacy for short-term political gain. The cumulative effect of such efforts, even when they are partially checked or prove temporary, is to undermine confidence that any institution can maintain genuine independence from political manipulation.

Protecting bridging institutions, therefore, requires architectural features that increase resilience against capture attempts while maintaining democratic accountability. This involves a delicate balance: bridging institutions need enough independence to resist immediate factional pressure while remaining ultimately accountable to public purposes rather than becoming unresponsive to legitimate democratic concerns. Various mechanisms contribute to this balance, including appointment processes that require cross-partisan consensus rather than simple majority control, term structures that prevent rapid turnover when political power shifts, professional qualification requirements that limit appointments to individuals with genuine relevant expertise, transparency rules that expose inappropriate political interference, and norm systems that impose reputational costs on actors who attempt blatant manipulation. None of these protections proves foolproof, and determined majorities can often overcome formal barriers. Still, they increase the costs and visibility of capture attempts, making them less attractive and easier for the public to recognize and resist.

Beyond formal institutional design, the architecture of trust requires attention to what might be called "verification ecosystems"—the networks of independent observers, journalists, researchers, auditors, and civil society organizations that monitor institutional performance and provide information allowing citizens to assess trustworthiness for themselves. These ecosystems serve as crucial intermediaries between complex institutions and ordinary citizens who lack the time and expertise to evaluate institutional performance directly. When verification ecosystems function effectively, they reduce information asymmetries, surface institutional failures before they become catastrophic, and create reputational incentives for institutional good behavior. When they fail or become captured by the same interests they should monitor, the information necessary for trust judgments becomes unavailable, and citizens must either grant unverified trust or assume the worst, neither of which supports healthy democratic function.

The fragmentation of verification ecosystems represents a particular challenge in contemporary fractured societies, as different communities increasingly rely on separate information sources that provide radically different assessments of institutional performance and social reality. When different groups consume different media, trust different experts, and operate within different epistemological frameworks, they cannot agree even on basic facts about institutional behavior, making collective trust judgments impossible. One community sees institutional failure requiring reform, while another sees a partisan attack requiring defensive solidarity; one group sees evidence of bias, while another considers evidence of fairness; one faction accepts specific expert claims as authoritative, while another dismisses the same experts as compromised partisans. This fragmentation means that even genuine institutional improvements may not rebuild trust across divides because different groups cannot agree on whether improvements have occurred or whether institutional performance meets acceptable standards.

Reunifying fractured verification ecosystems proves exceptionally difficult because it requires rebuilding epistemic common ground—shared standards for evaluating evidence, shared authorities recognized as legitimate arbiters of factual disputes, and shared commitment to updating beliefs based on new information rather than fitting all evidence into predetermined narratives. This cannot happen through simple appeals to consume more diverse information sources, because individuals already distrust the alternative sources their opponents rely on and often see engagement with such sources as exposure to propaganda rather than as an opportunity to expand their perspective. Instead, rebuilding shared verification capacity requires reconstructing institutions and practices that command cross-cutting respect through demonstrated competence and fairness over sustained periods. This might include professional journalism that transparently distinguishes between reporting and analysis and genuinely seeks to present information fairly rather than advancing particular agendas; scientific and expert communities that transparently acknowledge uncertainty and error while explaining their methodologies accessibly; and civic organizations that build reputations for honest information provision regardless of political convenience.

The temporal dimension of trust architecture deserves particular attention because trust relationships develop slowly but can collapse rapidly, creating asymmetries that complicate reunification efforts. Building trust requires consistent positive experiences accumulated over time—repeated demonstrations of competence, fairness, and reliability that gradually build confidence in predictable behavior. This accumulation process cannot be rushed because trust fundamentally involves willingness to make oneself vulnerable based on expectations about others' future behavior, and such vulnerability makes sense only when sufficient evidence has accumulated to justify confidence. Destroying trust, conversely, can happen instantly through a single dramatic betrayal or gradually through accumulated disappointments that eventually exhaust the benefit of the doubt. This asymmetry means that the timeline for rebuilding trust after a collapse extends far beyond the immediate present, requiring sustained consistency over years or even decades before confidence can be restored.

The extended timelines required for trust reconstruction create profound political challenges because democratic political systems operate on much shorter cycles, putting pressure for visible results within electoral timeframes that exceed the actual timeframes over which trust develops. Political leaders undertaking institutional reforms aimed at rebuilding trust face the paradox that the benefits of their efforts may not materialize until long after they have left office. In contrast, the costs and disruptions of reform are felt immediately. This creates perverse incentives to favor symbolic gestures over structural changes, short-term tactical moves over long-term strategic investments, and communication campaigns over genuine accountability reforms. Overcoming these incentive problems requires either unusual political leadership willing to prioritize long-term institutional health over short-term political advantage or institutional innovations that protect reform efforts from immediate political reversal when power shifts.

Historical examples illuminate both the challenges and possibilities of reconstructing trust architecture after catastrophic collapse. Post-war Germany rebuilt institutional legitimacy through a constitutional design that created strong institutional independence, robust federalism that prevented excessive power concentration, independent courts with genuine authority to check government action, and a transparent historical reckoning that acknowledged past institutional failures rather than denying or minimizing them. This reconstruction process took decades and required sustained commitment across political transitions. Still, it ultimately produced institutions that command broad public confidence despite operating in a society with profound historical reasons for skepticism about institutional power. Similarly, post-apartheid South Africa created institutions explicitly designed to rebuild trust across racial divisions, including a Truth and Reconciliation Commission that prioritized acknowledgment of past atrocities over immediate punishment, constitutional protections against majoritarian domination, and independent institutions charged with monitoring human rights compliance. While these institutions face ongoing challenges and critics question whether they have fulfilled their promise, they represent serious architectural attempts to address trust deficits rather than merely hoping that time would heal divisions without structural intervention.

Contemporary examples of trust architecture experiments proliferate across scales and contexts, offering laboratories for understanding what approaches might support reunification in fractured societies. Participatory budgeting processes across cities create mechanisms for citizens to directly shape resource-allocation decisions, building trust through transparent involvement rather than merely accepting elite determinations. Citizen assemblies selected through random sortition bring together diverse individuals to deliberate on contentious issues, creating spaces where ordinary people across divisions can discover common ground and develop nuanced positions that pure adversarial politics obscures. Deliberative polling processes demonstrate that when citizens receive balanced information and the opportunity to discuss issues with diverse others, they often develop more complex and moderate views than those expressed in standard polling driven by immediate reactions. Platform cooperatives experiment with digital infrastructure owned and governed by users rather than extractive corporations, testing whether different ownership structures can create more trustworthy online environments. These experiments vary in success and scale, but collectively they represent architecture-level thinking about trust rather than merely psychological or communicative approaches.

The relationship between trust architecture and inequality deserves explicit examination because material disparities profoundly affect the possibilities for trust in ways that no amount of institutional design can fully compensate for. When basic resources are distributed highly unequally, when opportunities for security and advancement differ radically across groups, when some communities experience material abundance while others face systematic deprivation, the foundations for trust become unstable regardless of institutional fairness. People experiencing deprivation understandably question whether institutions truly serve public purposes when outcomes are so unequal. At the same time, those in privileged positions often cannot recognize how their position shapes their trust judgments. Trust requires sufficient mutual investment in shared systems, and all parties genuinely care about institutional integrity. Still, extreme inequality creates situations in which different groups have fundamentally divergent interests in either maintaining or disrupting existing arrangements. This suggests that trust architecture alone cannot reunify deeply fractured societies unless it is accompanied by attention to the material conditions that make trust relationships psychologically and practically possible across divisions.

The digital transformation of social interaction creates new challenges and possibilities for trust architecture that remain imperfectly understood. Digital communication enables coordination and information sharing at unprecedented scale and speed. Still, it also facilitates manipulation, the rapid spread of misinformation, and the reduction of social cues that facilitate trust judgments in face-to-face interaction. Online environments currently tend to accelerate trust collapse through features such as anonymity, which reduces accountability, algorithmic amplification of engaging but often misleading content, and echo chamber effects that separate people into parallel information environments. Yet digital systems also enable new forms of trust architecture, including reputation systems that provide surrogates for personal knowledge, transparency mechanisms that make institutional operations more visible, verification systems that help distinguish reliable from unreliable information, and coordination platforms that help dispersed actors work together toward shared goals. The architectural challenge involves designing digital environments that preserve the coordination benefits while mitigating the trust-corroding features, a challenge that requires both technical innovation and governance frameworks that align platform incentives with public purposes rather than purely commercial objectives.

Moving forward, the architectural perspective suggests that reunifying fractured societies requires simultaneous work across multiple levels and time scales. It demands immediate attention to visible institutional failures that corrode trust daily, sustained commitment to structural reforms that will not yield benefits for years or decades, creative experimentation with new institutional forms suited to contemporary challenges, and patient cultivation of norms and practices that support trustworthy behavior across institutions and individuals. This architecture must be robust enough to function despite continued disagreement, flexible enough to adapt as circumstances change, and legitimate enough that diverse communities recognize it as genuinely serving public purposes rather than merely expressing power relationships in institutional form. The challenge is immense, but understanding trust as an architectural phenomenon rather than simply an emotional or communicative one at least provides frameworks for thinking systematically about what reunification requires and how progress might be measured and sustained.

Chapter 8: Shared Visions, Common Dreams

The work of reunifying fragmented societies requires more than repairing broken connections, rebuilding institutional trust, or cultivating empathy across dividing lines. It demands something simultaneously more ethereal and more fundamental: the creation or rediscovery of collective visions that can capture the imagination of people standing on opposite sides of seemingly unbridgeable chasms. While we have explored the mechanics of dialogue, the architecture of trust, and the power of empathy to reconnect divided communities, these processes risk remaining technical exercises unless animated by compelling narratives of possible futures that diverse groups can genuinely share. The question of shared visions strikes at the deepest challenge facing fractured societies—how can communities that have come to see themselves as fundamentally incompatible nonetheless discover or construct common dreams capacious enough to accommodate their differences while providing direction and meaning to their collective existence?

The very notion of shared visions might seem impossibly utopian in an era when fundamental factual reality has become contested territory. How can we speak of common dreams when communities cannot even agree on what constitutes truth, when historical narratives diverge so dramatically that the past itself becomes a battlefield, when the present is experienced so differently by various groups that they might as well be inhabiting separate worlds? Yet this profound challenge is precisely why articulating shared visions becomes essential rather than optional. Societies do not reunify by pretending differences do not exist or by one side capitulating to the other's worldview. They reunify by discovering or constructing overarching frameworks of meaning and purpose large enough to contain their conflicts without being torn apart by them. These frameworks do not eliminate disagreement but provide context that makes disagreement productive rather than destructive, transforming opponents into fellow travelers engaged in a common journey even as they argue about the route.

History offers instructive examples of how shared visions have held diverse societies together during periods of intense stress. Consider the American founding, which occurred amid deep disagreements over the nature of government, the structure of society, slavery, and the relationship between states and federal authority. The genius of the constitutional framework lay not in resolving these conflicts but in creating a sufficiently compelling vision of republican self-government that groups with fundamentally different economic interests, regional identities, and moral convictions could nonetheless commit to the project. The vision was simultaneously concrete enough to generate actual institutions and flexible enough to accommodate vastly different interpretations. Slaveholding southerners and abolitionist northerners, agrarian populists and commercial elites, those who feared centralized power and those who believed in energetic government could all find themselves, however uncomfortably, within the same national story because the founding vision was capacious enough to contain their contradictions, at least temporarily.

The temporary nature of that containment is itself instructive. The American experience demonstrates that shared visions require ongoing renewal and reinterpretation to remain viable. By the mid-nineteenth century, the founding vision had stretched to the breaking point precisely because the unresolved question of slavery had grown too large to be contained within interpretive frameworks that allowed for fundamental disagreement. The Civil War represented not merely a political breakdown but the shattering of a shared vision that could no longer accommodate the moral contradictions it had always contained. What emerged after that catastrophe was neither a simple return to the founding vision nor its complete replacement, but a painful process of reconstructing national meaning—a process that remains incomplete over a century and a half later. This historical trajectory reveals an uncomfortable truth: shared visions are not permanent solutions to social division but temporary constructions that must be continuously renewed, and they can fail catastrophically when the tensions they contain exceed their capacity to provide coherent meaning.

Contemporary fractured societies face a particular challenge in constructing shared visions because the very mechanisms through which collective meaning-making traditionally occurred have themselves become sites of contestation. Religious institutions that once provided overarching narratives and moral frameworks now divide rather than unite, with different theological traditions offering incompatible visions of the good society. Educational systems that might cultivate shared civic identities instead become battlegrounds over whose version of history gets taught, whose stories matter, and which traditions deserve preservation. Media that could facilitate broad conversations instead fragment into echo chambers, reinforcing existing divisions. Political processes that might forge compromise visions through negotiation instead amplify the most extreme positions and punish bridge-building. Even language itself—the basic tool through which shared understanding is constructed—has become weaponized, with identical terms carrying completely different meanings across communities. How do societies articulate shared visions when the very institutions and processes for doing so have been compromised?

The challenge becomes even more acute when we recognize that many current divisions reflect not merely different tactical preferences or interest group conflicts but genuinely incompatible moral visions. Consider debates about abortion, where one side understands the issue as a matter of women's bodily autonomy and individual liberty. At the same time, the other perceives it as involving the fundamental right to life of unborn children. No amount of dialogue or empathy eliminates this fundamental incompatibility—both sides are defending what they perceive as non-negotiable moral absolutes. Similarly, conflicts over religious liberty versus LGBTQ rights often involve fundamentally different conceptions of human dignity, moral authority, and social obligation, making reconciliation difficult. Environmental debates increasingly pit those who see climate change as an existential threat requiring immediate, dramatic action against those who prioritize economic development and individual freedom or who process scientific evidence through different epistemic frameworks. These are not conflicts that can be easily compromised because they involve competing visions of what it means to live well, what obligations we owe each other, and what kind of society we want to build.

Yet the inability to resolve these fundamental disagreements does not search for shared visions pointless; it makes that search more essential. The question is not how to create visions that eliminate moral disagreement—an impossible and probably undesirable goal—but how to construct frameworks of meaning that can accommodate fundamental differences while still providing sufficient common ground for coexistence and cooperation. This requires a shift in how we think about shared visions themselves. Rather than imagining them as comprehensive ideologies to which everyone must subscribe, we might conceive of shared visions as meta-frameworks that define the terms of engagement for communities that disagree profoundly about substance. A shared vision in this sense would not tell us how to resolve the abortion debate or reconcile religious liberty with LGBTQ rights, but it would establish that both sides have legitimate standing in our society, that both deserve to be heard, that neither can impose its view through raw power, and that our everyday life must somehow make space for this ongoing tension.

The construction of such meta-frameworks requires drawing on deeper wells of meaning that transcend particular policy disputes. One powerful source is the notion of dignity—the idea that every human being possesses inherent worth that must be recognized and respected regardless of their identity, beliefs, or circumstances. While communities disagree about what dignity requires in specific situations, the fundamental commitment to human dignity as a foundational value can serve as common ground even amid profound disagreement. Similarly, concepts like justice, despite being interpreted differently across communities, nonetheless provide shared vocabulary and shared aspirations that make a genuine argument possible. When both sides of a debate appeal to justice, they are at least operating within a common framework of moral discourse, even if they disagree about what justice requires. These shared aspirations—dignity, justice, liberty, community, security—function not as answers to our disputes but as the common language within which our conflicts can be productively conducted.

Another crucial dimension of viable shared visions involves narratives about collective identity that can incorporate diverse communities while still providing coherent meaning. National stories that function well in diverse societies tend to be structured around processes and principles rather than specific outcomes or particular cultural content. The American civil rights movement succeeded partly because it could frame its demands not as a request for special treatment but as a call to fulfill the nation's founding promises of equality and justice. Martin Luther King Jr.'s genius lay precisely in articulating Black liberation within a larger American dream that could, at least theoretically, encompass everyone. This strategic framing did not eliminate resistance nor resolve all contradictions, but it provided a vision that could bring diverse constituencies into a shared moral universe. Contemporary movements for reunification face similar challenges: how to articulate visions that honor particular identities and experiences while connecting them to larger stories about collective becoming that others can also inhabit.

The challenge of constructing such inclusive narratives is particularly acute in societies with histories of exclusion, oppression, and violence. Indigenous communities whose lands were stolen, ethnic minorities who faced systematic discrimination, religious groups that experienced persecution, and gender and sexual minorities subjected to legal and social marginalization. These groups reasonably ask why they should embrace shared visions with communities that excluded them from the original national story or that continue to deny the full gravity of historical injustices. The temptation toward separatism becomes understandable when the dominant narrative has never truly made space for your community's experience and when calls for unity often mean subordinating your concerns to supposedly more universal priorities. Any viable shared vision for societies with such histories must therefore incorporate rather than gloss over these painful realities. It must be capacious enough to include narratives of both national achievement and national failure, to honor both the ideals we claim and our profound betrayals of those ideals, and to recognize that, for many communities, the story of this society has been one of struggle against, not only within, the dominant frameworks.

Practical examples of how such inclusive visions can be constructed and sustained offer valuable guidance. Consider the case of Canada, which has struggled with deep divisions between Anglophone and Francophone communities, between indigenous peoples and settler societies, and between regions with dramatically different economic interests and cultural identities. While Canada's success at managing these tensions should not be overstated—significant conflicts and grievances persist—the country has nonetheless developed specific frameworks that allow for genuine difference while maintaining sufficient cohesion. Official bilingualism, constitutional recognition of multiple founding peoples, asymmetric federalism that allows Quebec different powers than other provinces, formal acknowledgment of indigenous sovereignty, and an explicit commitment to multiculturalism as a national value—these structural features embody a shared vision that is more about creating space for difference than imposing uniformity. The Canadian vision, to the extent it functions effectively, says: we are a society composed of multiple peoples with different languages, traditions, and aspirations, and our unity lies not in becoming the same but in our commitment to working out the terms of our ongoing coexistence through negotiation rather than domination.

Similarly instructive is the European Union project, which emerged from the catastrophic divisions of World War II with an explicit vision of making future wars impossible through economic integration and political cooperation. The EU's founding vision was not cultural homogenization or political centralization but rather the creation of frameworks that would make formerly hostile nations so interdependent that conflict would become unthinkable. This vision has faced severe stress in recent years, with Brexit representing its most dramatic rejection and various nationalist movements challenging its legitimacy. Yet the EU experience demonstrates that shared visions can work even when national identities remain, and substantial policy disagreements persist. The vision operates at a different level than daily political disputes, providing overarching purposes—peace, prosperity, cooperation—that diverse nations can support even while arguing about specific policies, institutional structures, or the appropriate balance between national sovereignty and collective governance.

These international examples highlight an essential principle: shared visions need not—and probably should not—be maximalist projects that attempt to specify every dimension of collective life. The totalizing ideologies of the twentieth century—fascism and communism—demonstrated the dangers of comprehensive visions that tried to organize every aspect of society around a single principle or goal. More viable are what might be called "thin" shared visions that establish fundamental commitments and frameworks while leaving substantial space for pluralism and disagreement within those frameworks. A thin shared vision might commit to democratic decision-making, constitutional limits on power, fundamental human rights, and peaceful conflict resolution while remaining agnostic about religion, cultural practices, economic organization beyond certain baseline protections, and many other dimensions of social life. The thinness is not a weakness but a strength, because it allows people with fundamentally different comprehensive worldviews to inhabit the same political space nonetheless.

The construction of such thin shared visions requires what political philosopher John Rawls termed "overlapping consensus"—the idea that people can support the same political principles for different reasons rooted in their distinct comprehensive doctrines. A Christian might support human rights because they believe humans are created in God's image. In contrast, a secular humanist supports the same rights based on the inherent dignity of autonomous rational beings, and a Buddhist supports them from convictions about universal compassion and the reduction of suffering. They arrive at similar political commitments through different philosophical or theological routes, and the shared vision does not require them to agree on ultimate foundations, only on the practical framework those foundations support. This approach has profound implications for reunification work because it suggests we need not resolve our deepest metaphysical or theological disagreements to construct common civic ground. The shared vision operates at a different level, one where our diverse comprehensive worldviews can reach overlapping conclusions even if they never converge completely.

Economic visions constitute another crucial dimension of this work, particularly because economic anxiety and inequality often drive social fragmentation. Communities cannot sustain shared political visions when they experience the economy in fundamentally different ways—when some see prosperity while others do not. At the same time, others face decline when economic gains concentrate in specific regions or demographic groups. In contrast, others are left behind when the future appears full of opportunity to some and threatening to others. Compelling shared visions must therefore include economic narratives that diverse communities can find credible and that offer plausible pathways to dignity and security for people in different circumstances. This does not require everyone to embrace the same economic ideology, but it does require frameworks that prevent economic differences from completely overwhelming other sources of solidarity. The New Deal in America functioned this way, providing a shared vision of economic security and opportunity that could unite industrial workers and farmers, immigrants and native-born citizens, diverse regions and industries around common projects of recovery and reform. While that particular coalition eventually fractured, its success in providing direction and meaning during a crisis illustrates how economic visions can contribute to broader social cohesion.

Contemporary efforts to articulate shared visions must also grapple with genuinely novel challenges that lack historical precedent. Climate change presents a particularly complex challenge because it requires coordinated action and sacrifice over long time horizons for diffuse benefits. In contrast, its costs and benefits are unequally distributed across regions, industries, and generations. Constructing shared visions of climate action requires bridging not only current political divisions but also generational divides and global inequalities between nations that industrialized early and those that are still developing. Technological transformation—artificial intelligence, biotechnology, automation, surveillance capabilities—creates similar challenges, requiring societies to develop shared frameworks for governing technologies whose implications we only partially understand and about which we have profound disagreements. These novel challenges cannot be addressed through a simple revival of older shared visions; they require the construction of new frameworks capable of organizing collective action around problems our ancestors never imagined.

The tension between aspirational ideals and realistic assessments is productive in developing shared visions. On one hand, compelling visions must inspire and motivate, pointing toward futures significantly better than the present and capable of capturing moral imagination. The civil rights movement's "beloved community," Lincoln's vision of a nation dedicated to the proposition that all people are created equal, the founding vision of a society based on self-government rather than hereditary privilege—these aspirational ideals mobilized collective action precisely because they transcended present realities and pointed toward transformative possibilities. Yet visions disconnected from realistic assessment of constraints, challenges, and human limitations often generate cynicism and disillusionment when reality fails to match rhetoric. The challenge is to construct visions that are simultaneously aspirational enough to inspire and realistic enough to guide actual decision-making, that acknowledge both our highest possibilities and our recurring failures, and that generate hope without descending into naivety.

The question of who gets to articulate shared visions and how they emerge is itself fraught with difficulty. In deeply divided societies, each community suspects that visions articulated by others are merely disguised attempts at domination, ways of imposing particular group interests or worldviews under the cover of universalism. This suspicion is often justified—historically, supposedly universal visions have frequently excluded or marginalized significant segments of society while presenting particular perspectives as neutral or natural. Women were excluded from founding visions of democratic citizenship, racial minorities from national stories, and religious minorities from civic participation, all while the dominant narratives presented themselves as encompassing everyone. Contemporary efforts to articulate shared visions must therefore be genuinely inclusive in their construction, involving diverse voices not as token representation but as co-creators whose perspectives fundamentally shape the emerging framework. This requires processes that distribute power more equitably than traditional forms of agenda-setting and narrative construction, that create space for perspectives that challenge dominant assumptions, and that remain open to ongoing revision rather than treating any articulated vision as final or complete.

Yet the challenge of inclusion creates its own difficulties, because genuinely inclusive processes that honor all perspectives may never reach consensus on anything substantive. If every stakeholder has veto power, if every perspective must be fully accommodated, and if no hierarchy of concerns or principles can be established, the result is likely paralysis rather than a functional shared vision. There is an unavoidable tension between inclusive processes and decisive outcomes, between honoring all voices and actually articulating coherent direction. Navigating this tension requires both procedural commitments—ensuring diverse participation, creating genuine opportunities for influence, distributing power more equitably—and substantive commitments to certain baseline principles that are not up for negotiation. A shared vision might be constructed through highly inclusive processes while nonetheless establishing that specific commitments—human dignity, democratic governance, fundamental rights—are foundational and non-negotiable, not because any particular group imposed them but because they represent necessary conditions for the kind of society that can actually sustain pluralism.

The work of constructing and sustaining shared visions also requires attention to the aesthetic and symbolic dimensions of collective life, rather than to abstract principles or policy frameworks. Shared visions become real and powerful partly through symbols, narratives, rituals, and aesthetic expressions that embody abstract commitments in tangible forms that can move hearts as well as convince minds. National flags, anthems, holidays, monuments, founding documents, sacred texts, cultural practices—these symbolic resources provide concrete manifestations of shared identity and common purpose. Yet in divided societies, these symbols themselves often become contested, with different communities interpreting them differently or rejecting them entirely as representing only dominant group perspectives. Confederate monuments in American communities, the presence of religious symbols in the public spaces of officially secular states, and national holidays that commemorate events differently across communities—these symbolic conflicts reflect more profound disagreements about collective identity and memory. Constructing viable shared visions requires either developing new symbols that can genuinely encompass diverse communities or reinterpreting existing symbols in ways that make space for multiple perspectives and experiences, acknowledging both what they represent to different groups and how they can function as familiar touchstones despite different interpretations.

Educational institutions play a particularly crucial role in sustaining shared visions across generations by introducing young people to collective narratives, historical memories, civic identities, and frameworks for understanding their society. Yet education has become one of the most contested arenas precisely because what gets taught, which stories get told, whose perspectives get centered, and which frameworks get employed all involve fundamental choices about collective identity and direction. History curricula that emphasize national achievements rather than foreground historical injustices, civics education that stresses common identity rather than highlighting ongoing exclusions, and literature selections that reflect diverse voices rather than focus on canonical texts—these pedagogical choices embody different visions of what the rising generation should understand about their society. Rather than viewing these conflicts as necessarily destructive, we might recognize them as opportunities to negotiate shared visions that genuinely encompass multiple perspectives. Educational frameworks that teach young people to hold complexity, to understand the same events from various vantage points, to recognize both achievements and failures in their society's history, to see themselves as inheritors of both ideals and unfinished business—such approaches might cultivate the capacity for the thinking shared visions require, where common commitments and ongoing disagreements coexist productively rather than destructively.

The temporal dimensions of shared visions require careful attention because fractured societies often divide in part around different relationships to the past, present, and future. Some communities may strongly orient toward preserving traditions and inherited ways of life, viewing rapid change as threatening and seeking visions that emphasize continuity with the past. Others may focus on rectifying historical injustices and constructing futures fundamentally different from what came before, experiencing traditional frameworks as oppressive and seeking visions that emphasize transformation and liberation. Still others may be primarily focused on present security and stability, suspicious of both backward-looking nostalgia and forward-looking utopianism. Compelling shared visions must somehow accommodate these different temporal orientations, honoring both continuity and change, both tradition and innovation, both historical memory and future aspiration. This requires narratives that connect past, present, and future in ways that allow people with different temporal orientations to find themselves in the same story— narratives that acknowledge what previous generations built while also recognizing their failures and limitations, that honor persistence of identity through time while also making space for evolution and growth.

Ultimately, the work of constructing shared visions for fractured societies is not a one-time achievement but an ongoing process of negotiation, articulation, and renewal that must occur across multiple dimensions simultaneously. It requires attention to abstract principles and concrete symbols, to inclusive processes and decisive outcomes, to aspirational ideals and realistic constraints, to continuity and change, to what unites us and what divides us. The goal is not eliminating difference or achieving complete consensus but rather constructing frameworks capacious enough to contain our conflicts without being destroyed by them, providing sufficient common ground for coexistence and cooperation while making space for genuine pluralism and ongoing disagreement. When these shared visions function effectively, they allow us to argue passionately about matters we care deeply about while still recognizing our opponents as legitimate participants in a common project rather than enemies to be vanquished. They transform zero-sum conflicts, where one side's victory requires the other's total defeat, into positive-sum challenges, where we succeed or fail together even as we disagree about strategy, priorities, and values. They create the possibility of genuinely diverse societies rather than merely fragmented, where difference enriches rather than threatens our collective life because an overarching framework of meaning and purpose holds those differences in productive rather than destructive tension. The work is never complete; the visions require constant renewal, and the challenges evolve as societies change. But without this ongoing effort to articulate what we share amid all that divides us, reunification remains impossible, and our conflicts will continue to tear us apart rather than challenge us to build something better together.

Chapter 9: The Healing of Communities

While the preceding explorations have addressed the conceptual, structural, and psychological dimensions of reunification, healing occurs not in abstractions but in concrete communities—geographically bounded or interest-defined groupings where people encounter one another in the recurring patterns of daily life. Communities represent the scale at which principles meet practice, where theories of reconciliation face the messy reality of neighbors who still carry grudges, local institutions bearing the scars of old conflicts, and social networks fractured by years of accumulated mistrust. The healing of communities involves transforming these immediate environments where division manifests most tangibly, creating spaces where the theoretical possibilities of reunification become lived realities for people whose daily routines bring them into unavoidable contact with those from whom they have been estranged.

What distinguishes community healing from broader societal reconciliation is its fundamentally spatial and relational character. A community exists in specific places—neighborhoods, towns, religious congregations, professional associations, schools, or online networks with stable membership—where the same individuals encounter one another repeatedly over extended periods. This geographic or social proximity means that unresolved conflicts cannot simply be avoided indefinitely; they persist as ongoing sources of discomfort, dysfunction, and reduced collective capacity. Unlike national or international divisions, where opponents might never meet face-to-face, community-level fractures create daily awkwardness, practical obstacles, and constant reminders of broken relationships. The divorced couple who must navigate school events for their children, the congregation split over theological or political issues where former friends now sit on opposite sides of the sanctuary, the neighborhood association paralyzed by factions that cannot agree on basic maintenance decisions—these situations demand resolution not primarily for abstract moral reasons but because persistent conflict makes ordinary life exhausting and collective action nearly impossible.

The intensity and unavoidability of community-level conflict paradoxically create both special difficulties and unique opportunities for healing. The problems arise from the accumulated weight of specific incidents, personal betrayals, and intimate knowledge of one another's flaws. At the community scale, conflicts are not abstract disagreements between demographic categories or political tribes but intensely personal wounds inflicted by known individuals whose faces, voices, and histories are intimately familiar. The business partner who betrayed a trust, the neighbor who called the police over a minor dispute, the school board member whose decision adversely affected one's child, the friend who posted something hurtful on social media—these are not distant others but people whose presence intrudes regularly into one's life. This proximity to harm-doers makes forgiveness psychologically more demanding even as it makes avoidance practically impossible. Yet this same intimacy creates opportunities absent in larger-scale reconciliation efforts. Community members share histories that predate their current conflicts, remember times when relationships worked, and have concrete stakes in whether their shared spaces function well. These accumulated connections provide materials for reconstruction that abstract citizens of divided nations lack.

The process of community healing typically begins not with grand gestures or formal ceremonies but with the restoration of minimal functional relationships that allow collective life to proceed. Before former adversaries can achieve anything resembling genuine reconciliation, they often must first establish what might be called "working coexistence"—the ability to participate together in essential community functions without the conflict paralyzing every interaction. This might mean developing protocols for running contentious meetings that prevent them from devolving into shouting matches, creating structured roles in community organizations that distribute power in ways all factions can accept, or simply establishing norms around which topics are temporarily off-limits in specific contexts. A community theater group torn apart by political divisions might agree that rehearsals will focus exclusively on the artistic work, channeling conflicts into designated discussion times when they cannot be avoided entirely. A neighborhood struggling with tensions between long-time residents and newcomers might establish a shared community garden where participation in the concrete work of planting and harvesting creates interaction around a neutral common project. These are not yet healing in any profound sense. Still, they establish the minimal conditions—regular constructive contact, successful completion of shared tasks, demonstration that cooperation remains possible—upon which more profound reconciliation might eventually build.

The geography and physical infrastructure of communities play crucial roles in either facilitating or obstructing healing processes. Divided communities often develop spatial patterns that reflect and reinforce their fractures: neighborhoods where different groups cluster separately, community facilities that become identified with particular factions, and public spaces that specific populations avoid because they feel unwelcome or unsafe. These patterns create parallel worlds in which groups lead substantially separate lives despite nominal residence in the same community, each developing narratives, norms, and institutions that increasingly diverge over time. Healing such communities requires intentional attention to spatial design and the use of physical infrastructure to create opportunities for contact that would not occur organically. This might involve locating new community facilities—libraries, recreation centers, health clinics—in neutral territories or deliberately on boundaries between divided areas, designing them to attract multiple groups and create natural opportunities for interaction. It might mean reimagining the use of existing spaces, transforming a parking lot into a pedestrian plaza where different community members naturally encounter one another, or converting an abandoned building into a community center deliberately designed to host activities that appeal across dividing lines. The principle is that physical space is never neutral; it either reinforces separation or creates opportunities for connection, and communities serious about healing must intentionally shape their built environment to support the relationships they wish to cultivate.

Economic dimensions profoundly influence community healing trajectories in ways that purely cultural or political approaches often overlook. Many community divisions have economic roots or dimensions—gentrification pitting long-time residents against newcomers, plant closures creating resentment between workers and management, development projects dividing those who might benefit economically from those who fear displacement or environmental harm. Attempting to heal such communities without addressing these material realities typically fails because the underlying sources of conflict remain active. Successful community healing in economically divided contexts often requires creating institutional mechanisms that distribute economic benefits more equitably or provide all groups with meaningful stakes in collective prosperity. A community torn by gentrification might establish community land trusts that preserve affordable housing while allowing development, giving both existing residents security and newcomers places to live. A town divided over industrial development might create benefit-sharing agreements ensuring that economic gains flow to all segments of the community rather than accumulating with property owners or outside investors. These approaches recognize that while economic disputes cannot be reduced to mere material calculations, they always carry cultural meanings and trigger psychological responses—neither can they be resolved through dialogue alone without addressing the actual distribution of resources and opportunities that fuel ongoing resentment.

The role of community institutions—schools, religious organizations, civic associations, local businesses, and media—proves decisive in determining whether healing occurs or divisions calcify. These institutions serve as the infrastructure of community life, shaping who encounters whom, what issues receive attention, which voices get amplified, and how conflicts get addressed or ignored. In divided communities, institutions often become captured by one faction, perceived as biased, or paralyzed by the need to avoid controversy, losing their capacity to serve integrative functions. Healing requires either reforming existing institutions to become genuinely inclusive or creating new ones that can bridge divides that older institutions cannot cross. This institutional work differs from mere structural reform because it must attend not just to formal rules and procedures but to the subtle cultural norms, interpersonal networks, and symbolic meanings that determine whether diverse community members actually feel welcome and whether institutions genuinely serve integrative purposes. A community center that technically offers equal access to all groups but whose programming, aesthetic, and staff communicate that it really belongs to a particular demographic will not serve healing functions. A school that formally celebrates diversity but whose disciplinary practices disproportionately impact specific populations will reinforce rather than bridge divisions. Institutional healing requires this deeper work of transformation, changing not just policies but organizational cultures, not just stated values but daily practices that communicate who actually matters and belongs.

Generational dynamics create both complications and opportunities for community healing that differ markedly from individual reconciliation processes. Communities contain multiple generations simultaneously, each carrying different memories of conflict, different degrees of investment in old grievances, and different openness to reconciliation. Older generations who directly experienced the events that fractured the community often carry the deepest wounds and strongest attachments to particular narratives of what happened and who deserves blame. Middle generations may be somewhat more open to reconciliation, especially if they perceive continuing division as harming their children or limiting their community's potential. Younger generations who did not directly experience the original conflicts may be most open to healing. Yet, they inherit the consequences of divisions they did not create—segregated schools, limited opportunities, truncated social networks—and may resent both the conflicts and the expectation that they should participate in healing them. Successful community healing strategies recognize these generational differences and work simultaneously on multiple time scales. This might mean creating spaces where elders can share their stories and receive acknowledgment, while also developing programs that engage youth in shared projects unrelated to historical grievances. It might involve explicitly preparing younger generations to assume leadership in communities still shaped by older conflicts, equipping them with the skills to manage inherited tensions without being imprisoned by them. The goal is not erasing generational memory but transforming what gets transmitted—shifting from the inheritance of enmity to the inheritance of hard-won wisdom about how communities can navigate profound difference.

The phenomenon of what might be termed "small wins" plays an outsized role in community healing processes, providing concrete evidence that change is possible and building momentum for more ambitious efforts. Unlike national reconciliation processes that might unfold over decades with uncertain outcomes, community-level healing can sometimes demonstrate visible progress relatively quickly when the right opportunities emerge and leadership channels energy effectively. A successful joint project between formerly antagonistic groups—a community cleanup, a fundraiser for a shared cause, a cultural celebration that genuinely brings diverse residents together—can shift atmospheres more dramatically than its modest scale might suggest. These small wins work their healing effects through multiple mechanisms: they provide positive shared experiences that create new memories to compete with negative ones, they demonstrate that cooperation is practically possible even when trust remains limited, they identify individuals willing to take risks for reconciliation who might form the core of broader efforts, and they offer evidence that investment in healing work produces tangible returns. Communities need not wait for comprehensive solutions to all their divisions before beginning healing; they can start with whatever project or issue offers sufficient common ground and build outward from initial successes. The key is recognizing these small wins when they occur, celebrating them appropriately, analyzing what made them successful, and deliberately designing next steps that expand the circle of participation and deepen engagement.

The challenge of commemorative practices and historical narratives constitutes one of the most sensitive dimensions of community healing. Divided communities inevitably carry conflicting stories about the events that fractured them, with different groups remembering different aspects, emphasizing different causes, and identifying different villains and victims. These competing narratives are not merely intellectual disagreements but repositories of pain, vehicles for teaching identity to younger generations, and justifications for present-day positions and demands. Traditional approaches to this challenge have typically taken one of two forms: attempting to establish a single "true" narrative that everyone should accept, or avoiding historical questions entirely by focusing exclusively on the future. Neither approach works well in practice. Imposing a single narrative typically means privileging one group's memory over others, creating resentment, and ensuring that suppressed counter-narratives will resurface to challenge official histories. Avoiding history altogether leaves wounds unacknowledged, lessons unlearned, and the past constantly intruding into present debates because it was never adequately addressed. More successful approaches involve what might be called "narrative integration"—not forced agreement on a single story but the development of community practices that allow multiple stories to be told, heard, and held together in productive tension. This might take the form of community history projects that deliberately document diverse perspectives, memorial practices that acknowledge complexity rather than offering simple hero-and-villain narratives, or educational approaches that teach students to understand how reasonable people can interpret the same events differently based on their positions and experiences. The goal is not to eliminate differences in historical understanding but to create communities capable of living with them without letting them reignite conflict.

Leadership for community healing requires capabilities distinct from those in other contexts, combining features of facilitation, conflict mediation, project management, and political organizing while demanding unusual emotional intelligence and moral credibility. Effective healing leaders must be able to maintain relationships across dividing lines simultaneously, which often means absorbing criticism and suspicion from all sides as they work to build bridges. They must be able to hold long-term visions of reconciliation while managing the pragmatic work of small incremental steps, neither becoming so idealistic that they lose touch with what is practically achievable nor becoming so focused on immediate tasks that they lose sight of ultimate purposes. They need sufficient power and position to access resources and command attention, but not so much power that they dominate processes that require broad ownership and participation. Perhaps most challenging, they must navigate the tension between neutrality and advocacy—remaining sufficiently impartial to be trusted as facilitators while being adequately committed to justice that they do not simply preserve existing power arrangements under the guise of reconciliation. These leadership demands mean that community healing rarely depends on a single heroic individual but typically requires teams or networks of leaders representing different constituencies, bringing diverse capabilities, and sharing the burdens of this demanding work. The development and support of such leadership are crucial tasks in themselves, requiring training programs, peer networks, and institutional roles that give healing work the resources and legitimacy it needs to succeed.

The relationship between community healing and broader justice concerns generates ongoing tensions that must be navigated rather than resolved definitively. In many divided communities, fractures arose from or were deepened by injustices—discriminatory practices, unequal resource distribution, incidents of violence or exploitation—that remain unaddressed or inadequately remedied. Pushing too quickly toward reconciliation without adequate attention to justice can feel like demanding that victims forgive and forget while the conditions that enabled their victimization persist. Yet insisting on complete justice before any reconciliation can begin often proves impossible because fractured communities rarely agree on what justice requires, who deserves it, or who should provide it. This impasse has led some healing practitioners toward what might be called "justice-in-process" approaches that view healing and justice not as sequential stages but as intertwined practices pursued simultaneously. This means combining acknowledgment of past wrongs with concrete steps toward changed conditions, formal recognition of harm with practical efforts toward restoration, and historical memory work with forward-looking institutional reform. A community addressing historic discrimination might simultaneously pursue reparative economic programs, educational initiatives that teach accurate history, and dialogue processes that allow those harmed to share their experiences and those implicated to grapple with responsibility. No single initiative satisfies all justice demands, but the combination demonstrates seriousness about addressing wrongs while creating space for relationships to begin healing.

The digital dimension of contemporary community life creates unprecedented challenges and opportunities for healing that previous generations of community workers never faced. Many communities now exist partly or entirely in digital spaces—online forums, social media groups, virtual communities of interest or identity—where traditional spatial dynamics do not apply. Yet, conflicts and fractures arise just as they do in physical communities. Moreover, physical communities now have digital lives through neighborhood social media groups, local online forums, and digital communication channels that profoundly shape how community members interact, perceive issues, and organize. These digital dimensions complicate healing in obvious ways. For example, anonymity and distance make cruelty easier, algorithms often amplify divisive content, and the permanence of online communication means that hurtful statements can be revisited indefinitely. Yet digital tools also create healing possibilities: they allow connection across physical distances, enable forms of expression that might be difficult face-to-face, provide platforms for marginalized voices to be heard, and create records that can support accountability. Communities pursuing healing increasingly need digital strategies as sophisticated as their physical ones, thinking intentionally about how online spaces are designed and moderated, how digital communication either reinforces or bridges divisions, and how virtual and physical community life can be integrated rather than allowed to develop as separate realities with different norms and different populations.

The question of sustainability haunts community healing efforts because the conditions that initially fractured communities rarely disappear permanently, and the hard work of reconciliation can unravel if not continuously maintained. Communities that achieve significant healing often discover that new conflicts arise, external pressures revive old divisions, generational turnover means that lessons learned are not automatically transmitted, or simple fatigue causes engagement with healing work to decline. Sustainable healing requires institutionalization—embedding practices, structures, and norms developed during intensive healing periods into the community's ongoing life so they persist when special attention fades. This might mean transforming temporary conflict-resolution processes into permanent community institutions, incorporating dialogue practices into the standard operating procedures of community organizations, or creating community positions explicitly tasked with maintaining relationships across divisions and addressing emerging conflicts before they escalate. It also requires what might be called "healing traditions"—regular practices, rituals, and commemorations that continuously rehearse the community's commitment to bridging differences, recall its history of overcoming conflicts, and reintegrate members who have become alienated. A community that successfully navigated a bitter division might establish an annual event celebrating that achievement, not as triumphalism but as a reminder and renewal of the commitments that made healing possible. The principle is that healing is not a destination but a practice, not something achieved once and finished, but something requiring continuous attention and periodic renewal.

The healing of communities ultimately depends on cultivating what might be termed "relational infrastructure"—the networks of relationships, practices of interaction, and norms of engagement that determine how community members treat one another and how conflicts get addressed. Physical infrastructure, like roads and buildings, decays without maintenance and must be continuously renewed; relational infrastructure functions similarly, requiring ongoing investment and attention to remain functional. In fractured communities, this relational infrastructure has often deteriorated profoundly—former friends no longer speak, traditional sites of gathering have become contested or abandoned, norms of civility and mutual respect have broken down, and the social capital that once allowed the community to address challenges collectively has been depleted. Healing requires rebuilding this infrastructure, which proves more difficult than constructing physical facilities because relationships cannot be engineered or commanded into existence. They must be grown slowly through repeated positive interactions, demonstrated reliability, and accumulated experiences of mutual support. This work requires patience, perseverance, and a willingness to invest in processes whose outcomes cannot be precisely predicted or controlled. Yet without this relational infrastructure, communities remain vulnerable to fracturing under any significant stress, unable to mobilize collective resources to address challenges, and incapable of providing the social support and sense of belonging that makes life meaningful. The healing of communities is ultimately the reconstruction of this relational infrastructure, creating conditions in which people with differences can nonetheless recognize their fundamental interdependence and treat one another with the dignity and respect that such recognition demands.

The temporal rhythms of community healing deserve closer attention than they typically receive in reconciliation literature. Communities operate according to natural cycles—seasonal changes, annual celebrations, recurring meetings and gatherings—that provide structure to collective life and create opportunities for healing interventions timed to these existing patterns. A community that experiences its worst divisions around budget season might deliberately introduce dialogue processes in advance of those annual conflicts, creating space to address underlying tensions before they manifest in their usual destructive forms. Religious communities might align reconciliation work with seasons already associated with reflection, forgiveness, and renewal in their traditions—such as Lent, Ramadan, and Yom Kippur—allowing healing efforts to draw on existing spiritual frameworks and communal practices. Secular communities might use anniversaries of significant events, whether traumatic or celebratory, as occasions for collective reflection on how far the community has come and what work remains to be done. These temporal strategies recognize that healing does not occur in abstract time but within the specific rhythms of particular communities, and that working with rather than against these rhythms can make healing efforts feel more natural and less imposed from outside.

The role of beauty and aesthetic experience in community healing represents an undertheorized dimension that practitioners often discover through experience, even when scholarly literature neglects it. Communities pursuing healing sometimes find that shared aesthetic experiences—musical performances, art installations, theatrical productions, festivals—create openings for connection that more explicitly reconciliation-focused activities cannot achieve. There is something about encountering beauty together, experiencing the transcendent or the delightful in company with others, including those from whom one has been divided, that can temporarily suspend hostilities and remind participants of their common humanity. A divided neighborhood might find that a community mural project, where residents work together to create something beautiful for their shared space, facilitates conversations and builds relationships in ways that formal dialogue sessions never could. A congregation split over painful issues might discover that singing together in worship creates a sense of unity that theological discussions only seem to threaten. These experiences do not resolve the underlying conflicts—the disagreements and grievances remain—but they provide evidence that division is not the only reality, that connection remains possible, and that the community can create something valuable together despite its fractures. This matters because healing requires not just resolving problems but also cultivating positive experiences that make continued investment in the community feel worthwhile. Communities cannot heal through conflict resolution alone; they must also create moments of joy, beauty, and transcendence that remind members why healing matters and what becomes possible when they manage to bridge their divisions.

The phenomenon of "healing leaders" emerging from unexpected quarters presents both opportunities and challenges for community reconciliation work. Sometimes the individuals most capable of bridging divides are not the prominent community leaders—the elected officials, organizational presidents, or long-established authorities— but somewhat relative newcomers, younger members, or people who occupied marginal positions within the community's pre-conflict structure. These unexpected leaders often possess advantages that established leaders lack: they may have fewer historical entanglements and grudges, less investment in maintaining positions that contribute to conflict, and more freedom to experiment with unconventional approaches. A community might find that healing work makes the most progress when led by someone who moved to town after the initial rupture and thus carries no personal history with the conflict, or by young adults whose generational position permits them to question patterns their elders take for granted. Yet this dynamic creates challenges around legitimacy and sustainability. Established leaders may resist or undermine initiatives led by those they perceive as lacking proper authority or understanding of community history. Healing efforts led by charismatic individuals without institutional backing may achieve impressive short-term results but fail to create lasting change because they depend too heavily on particular personalities. Successful community healing typically requires both the innovative energy that unexpected leaders often bring and the institutional legitimacy and resources that established authorities can provide, suggesting the importance of coalition leadership models that bring diverse voices into complementary roles rather than seeking a single healing champion.

Chapter 10: A New Dawn of Understanding

The journey from fragmentation to reunification traces an arc that begins with recognition of division, moves through the difficult work of repair, and arrives—if all goes well—at a transformed state where understanding itself has been fundamentally reconstituted. What we have explored thus far addresses the mechanisms, processes, and conditions that enable healing. Yet there comes a moment in any genuine reunification when something shifts at a deeper level, when the accumulated work of dialogue, bridge-building, empathy cultivation, trust reconstruction, and community healing produces not merely a patched-together society but an actual transformation in how people perceive themselves and their relationship to difference. This transformation represents what might be called a new dawn of understanding—not a return to some imagined harmony of the past, nor an erasure of the difficulties that produced fracture, but rather an emergent capacity to hold complexity, contradiction, and diversity within frameworks of meaning that enhance rather than diminish our collective life. Understanding at this level transcends mere tolerance of difference or resigned acceptance of pluralism; it encompasses a genuine reorientation of consciousness that allows us to experience diversity itself as generative rather than threatening, to perceive disagreement as potentially creative rather than inevitably destructive, and to recognize that the conflicts we cannot eliminate might nevertheless serve purposes we had not previously grasped. This chapter explores what such a transformed understanding looks like as it begins to dawn in societies that have undertaken the hard work of reunification, examining both the indicators that suggest genuine transformation rather than superficial accommodation and the conditions that allow this dawning to occur and spread throughout communities previously convinced of their irreconcilable differences.

The first and perhaps most subtle indication that understanding has genuinely transformed appears in how societies begin to narrate their own conflicts. In the early stages of division, communities typically construct their stories around clear heroes and villains, innocent victims and guilty perpetrators, reasonable positions and irrational extremism. These narratives provide psychological comfort and group cohesion, but they also lock societies into positions from which compromise appears as betrayal and complexity as confusion. As reunification work proceeds through the stages we have examined, something remarkable sometimes happens to these stories—not that they reverse or that groups suddenly adopt their opponents' narratives, but instead that the storytelling itself becomes more complex, more capable of holding multiple perspectives simultaneously, more willing to acknowledge that various groups experienced the same events in genuinely different ways that all contain elements of truth. This narrative sophistication goes far beyond rhetorical politeness or strategic ambiguity; it reflects a fundamental shift in how people understand causation, agency, and responsibility in social conflicts. When a society can tell stories about its divisions that acknowledge how good intentions produced terrible outcomes, how rational responses to genuine threats created new dangers, how victim and perpetrator categories prove inadequate to capture the recursive nature of conflict escalation, that society has achieved a level of understanding that makes genuine transformation possible. The narratives become capable of accommodating paradox rather than resolving everything into simple moral binaries, creating space for political and social arrangements that would be incomprehensible within the earlier, simpler frameworks.

This narrative transformation manifests most powerfully in how societies begin to commemorate their periods of division. Early in reunification processes, communities often find commemoration impossibly contentious—whose suffering will be acknowledged, whose heroes will be honored, whose version of events will become official history. These fights over memory can reignite conflicts that seemed to be healing, as each community fights to ensure its experience receives proper recognition. Yet when understanding has genuinely transformed, commemoration itself changes character. Rather than competing monuments that assert opposing truths, societies begin creating memorial spaces that acknowledge complexity, that honor suffering across dividing lines, that present historical events in ways that invite reflection rather than reinforcing group identities. Some of the most potent examples come from post-conflict societies that have created museums or memorial sites where visitors encounter multiple perspectives presented in ways that make clear the incompleteness of any single viewpoint. These spaces do not relativize suffering or suggest that all positions are equally valid; instead, they convey that the conflicts themselves are more complex than any simplified version can capture, and that understanding requires wrestling with contradictions rather than resolving them prematurely. When such commemorative practices become possible and even valued by communities that were recently in conflict, it signals that understanding has evolved to a point where people can tolerate the discomfort of complexity because they have discovered that simplistic clarity comes at too high a price. The society has learned, in effect, that some tensions must be maintained rather than resolved, that premature closure on difficult questions produces false peace that eventually collapses, and that the ability to hold multiple truths simultaneously represents maturity rather than confusion.

Another profound indicator of transformed understanding appears in how societies begin to approach education, particularly the formation of young people who will inherit the society that reunification efforts are attempting to create. In deeply divided societies, education typically becomes a battleground where different communities fight to ensure their versions of history, their values, and their worldviews receive proper representation or, failing that, to create separate educational systems that protect their children from contamination by opposing perspectives. As reunification progresses, initial steps often focus on reducing the most inflammatory elements of curricula, removing the most egregious vilification of opposing groups, and perhaps introducing some acknowledgment of multiple perspectives. These early reforms, while important, generally represent political compromises more than a genuine transformation of understanding. The dawn of new understanding becomes visible when educational approaches begin to embrace something more radical: the explicit teaching of perspectival thinking itself, the cultivation of capacities to inhabit multiple viewpoints, the development of comfort with ambiguity and paradox as fundamental intellectual skills rather than regrettable necessities. Schools in societies experiencing this transformation begin teaching not just that different groups interpret historical events differently, but why such differences emerge, how perspective shapes perception, what it means to hold space for contradictory truths, and how to make judgments in contexts where certainty remains elusive. This pedagogical shift reflects an understanding that the goal of education in diverse societies cannot be to transmit a single agreed-upon framework but rather to develop citizens capable of navigating difference, uncertainty, and complexity with sophistication and grace. When previously conflicting communities can agree on educational approaches that essentially teach their children to question all narratives, including their own, to recognize the constructed nature of all perspectives, including their own communities', and to develop genuine curiosity about radically different ways of understanding the world, something fundamental has shifted in how society understands the nature of understanding itself.

The transformation of understanding also manifests in evolving attitudes toward expertise and authority, particularly in how societies balance different forms of knowledge. Deeply divided societies often find themselves split not only over values and interests but over epistemology itself—over what counts as valid knowledge, who qualifies as a legitimate authority, and how conflicting truth claims should be adjudicated. Some communities privilege scientific expertise and empirical methodology, dismissing other ways of knowing as superstition or subjective opinion. Others emphasize traditional knowledge, lived experience, or spiritual insight, viewing exclusive reliance on scientific authority as a form of cultural imperialism or dehumanization. These epistemological divisions can prove even more intractable than disagreements over policies or resources, because they affect the very grounds on which disagreements might be resolved. When understanding begins to transform genuinely, societies develop more sophisticated approaches to these questions—not by declaring all forms of knowledge equally valid regardless of domain, which replaces one simplification with another, but by developing frameworks that recognize different questions require different forms of expertise, that various knowledge systems illuminate different dimensions of complex realities, and that the most robust understanding often emerges from dialogue between multiple epistemological traditions rather than victory of one over others. This epistemological maturity appears when, for example, environmental policy begins to integrate scientific data on ecosystems with traditional ecological knowledge held by indigenous communities, recognizing that these different knowledge systems are not simply competing but can be complementary, each seeing aspects of reality that the other misses. Similarly, in healthcare, societies experiencing a transformed understanding begin creating approaches that can hold space for evidence-based medicine alongside attention to the lived experience of illness, the cultural meanings of suffering, and the spiritual dimensions of healing, without collapsing these domains into one another or establishing artificial hierarchies among them. This epistemological sophistication represents a profound shift in understanding itself—a movement beyond both naive certainty and paralyzing relativism toward what might be called critical pluralism. This approach maintains standards of rigor and evidence while recognizing that reality is rich enough to sustain multiple valid but partial perspectives.

The dawn of transformed understanding particularly reveals itself in how societies begin to approach their most intractable disagreements—those conflicts that seem to admit no compromise because they involve fundamental values or identity commitments rather than merely distributable resources. In the earlier stages we have examined, such disagreements are typically managed tactically: groups agree to disagree, establish procedures for decision-making despite ongoing conflict, or create arrangements that allow different communities to pursue various approaches across domains. These procedural solutions provide stability and may prevent violence, but they generally do not represent a transformation of understanding so much as an agreement to contain its absence. Something genuinely new emerges when societies develop what might be called tragic wisdom regarding their deepest conflicts—an understanding that some disagreements cannot be resolved because they reflect genuinely incommensurable values or perspectives, that choosing one legitimate good sometimes requires sacrificing another legitimate good, that our social arrangements inevitably privilege some forms of life while constraining others, and that this reality calls not for increasingly clever solutions that promise to satisfy everyone but for cultivated sensibilities that can acknowledge loss, honor what must be relinquished, and distribute the burdens of irresolvable conflict with as much justice as possible. This tragic sensibility differs markedly from both optimistic narratives that promise win-win solutions to all disputes and pessimistic resignation that abandons the pursuit of justice altogether. It represents instead a mature realism that understands that societies will always face genuine dilemmas in which all available choices involve real costs, and that honoring competing goods requires not finding the option that avoids trade-offs but making trade-offs in ways that acknowledge their gravity and distribute their weight fairly. When abortion debates, for instance, evolve from absolutist assertions of either fetal rights or women's autonomy toward frameworks that acknowledge the genuine values at stake on all sides, accept that legal arrangements will inevitably privilege some values over others, and focus on minimizing harms and supporting those who bear the costs of whatever arrangements emerge, that represents transformed understanding even if the substantive disagreements remain. The transformation lies not in discovering answers that make everyone happy but in developing capacities to live together despite profound dispute in ways that honor the humanity of all parties and acknowledge the genuine moral weight of competing commitments.

This tragic wisdom extends to how transforming societies approach their past injustices and continuing inequalities. The earlier work of truth commissions, reparations debates, and structural reforms that we have touched upon represents crucial stages in addressing historical wrongs. Yet a new dawn of understanding brings something additional: recognition that no amount of acknowledgment, apology, or material redress can fully repair what was destroyed or restore what was lost. This recognition might seem pessimistic —a counsel of despair that suggests historical injustice cannot be addressed. In fact, it produces something quite different—a liberation from the impossible demand for complete restoration that allows societies to focus instead on what actually can be accomplished. When descendants of enslaved people and descendants of enslavers, for instance, move beyond the paralyzing question of whether any reparations could ever be adequate to the harm inflicted, they sometimes discover space for acknowledging that inadequacy need not preclude meaningful action, that partial justice remains worth pursuing even when perfect justice proves impossible, and that the work of repair has value independent of whether it can ever be completed. This shift in understanding allows formerly hostile parties to undertake ambitious programs of redress and transformation precisely because they have abandoned the fantasy that such programs might somehow make everything right, returning instead to the more modest but achievable goal of creating a future less disfigured by past injustice than the present remains. The new understanding recognizes that societies carry their histories forward in ways that cannot be undone, that present institutions and distributions of advantage reflect past injustices in ways that cannot be entirely disentangled, but that these realities make ongoing efforts at repair more rather than less necessary. When acknowledgment of irreparable harm leads not to paralysis but to sustained commitment to mitigating continuing effects, understanding has transformed in ways that make genuine reunification possible without requiring the impossible precondition of somehow escaping history.

The transformation of understanding also manifests in changed relationships to time and to the pace of change itself. Societies in the grip of intense conflict typically experience time in distorted ways—either racing urgently toward some decisive confrontation that will resolve matters once and for all, or stuck in what feels like endless cycling through the same conflicts without progress. The processes we have examined—dialogue, bridge-building, trust reconstruction—all require patience and sustained effort over extended periods, teaching societies that meaningful change operates on timelines measured in years and decades rather than news cycles or election seasons. Yet something additional happens when understanding genuinely transforms: societies develop what might be called temporal wisdom, an altered relationship to time that recognizes both the urgency of present suffering and the extended duration of genuine transformation, that can maintain commitment across leadership changes and political cycles, that understands that different aspects of reunification operate on different timescales requiring different strategies, and that becomes comfortable with the reality that the work of healing and reunification never reaches completion but requires ongoing renewal. This temporal wisdom appears when societies can simultaneously push for immediate reforms that address urgent injustices while maintaining decades-long commitments to institutional transformation that cannot be rushed, when they can mark progress in ways that sustain morale and commitment without demanding impossible speeds of change, and when they can accept that each generation must do its own work of reunification rather than imagining that one generation's efforts will somehow permanently resolve what humans have struggled with throughout history. Northern Ireland, for example, has demonstrated this temporal wisdom in maintaining peace process commitments through multiple governments and continuing periods of institutional difficulty, recognizing that the Good Friday Agreement represented not an endpoint but the beginning of a generations-long transformation. When societies can distinguish between the patience required for genuine transformation and the complacency that accepts unnecessary suffering, they have achieved an understanding of time that makes sustained reunification efforts possible without demanding superhuman persistence in the face of endless frustration.

Another dimension of transformed understanding appears in how societies rebuild their public spheres and information ecosystems. The fragmentation we examined earlier includes the breakdown of shared informational environments, with different communities inhabiting distinct factual universes, and the impossibility of democratic deliberation when citizens cannot agree on fundamental realities. Initial responses often focus on fact-checking, media literacy education, and technical solutions to misinformation—all valuable interventions that address critical problems. The new dawn of understanding, however, brings recognition that information problems in divided societies run deeper than simply false content or technical manipulation. What transforms is understanding of why certain narratives prove compelling to particular communities, how information consumption relates to identity and belonging, why fact-checking often backfires by strengthening the very beliefs it challenges, and what it means to create informational environments that serve diverse communities without fragmenting into completely separated realities. Societies experiencing this transformation begin developing communication infrastructures that explicitly acknowledge perspective and partiality rather than claiming impossible omniscience, that create spaces for engagement across difference without demanding premature consensus, that help people develop capacities to navigate information environments they know to be populated by actors with diverse agendas, and that understand that the goal cannot be creating a single authoritative source that everyone trusts but instead developing distributed networks of credibility that maintain sufficient overlap to enable collective decision-making. When news organizations, for instance, begin clearly identifying their reporting perspective while maintaining journalistic standards, acknowledging what they can and cannot know, presenting information in ways that invite audience members to engage critically rather than accept passively, and creating intentional opportunities for audiences to encounter perspectives they do not typically seek out, that represents transformed understanding of how information functions in diverse democracies. The transformation lies not in solving the problem of misinformation through technical means but in developing more sophisticated understandings of how knowledge, narrative, and identity interact, and creating communication practices adequate to those complexities.

The transformation of understanding fundamentally alters how societies approach leadership and political authority. In deeply divided contexts, leaders typically emerge by sharpening differences, mobilizing their base through clear opposition to the other side, and demonstrating strength through refusal to compromise on core commitments. The entire logic of political competition pushes toward polarization and away from the bridge-building and empathy we have examined as necessary for reunification. When understanding begins to transform genuinely, however, societies sometimes develop altered criteria for leadership that value different qualities—the ability to articulate collective goods that transcend partisan divisions, the courage to challenge one's own base when necessary for the common good, the wisdom to distinguish between principles requiring steadfastness and positions where flexibility serves larger purposes, and the humility to acknowledge uncertainty and to learn from opponents. This transformation in leadership values rarely happens through simple virtue ethics or exhortations for better character in politicians. Instead, it typically requires both cultural shifts in what publics reward and institutional reforms that change the incentives facing political actors, creating environments where bridge-building leadership becomes strategically viable rather than tantamount to political suicide. When electoral systems, media environments, and civic cultures evolve in ways that make it possible for leaders to build coalitions across dividing lines, to acknowledge complexity without appearing weak, to change positions in response to evidence without being destroyed for inconsistency, and to pursue incremental progress rather than promising revolutionary transformation, the understanding of leadership itself has transformed. New Zealand under Jacinda Ardern's early tenure, for example, demonstrated how leadership that emphasized collective wellbeing, acknowledged the limits of what government can accomplish, and explicitly reached across partisan divides could sometimes succeed even in contemporary political environments generally hostile to such approaches. When societies can reward such leadership rather than treating it as naive or weak, they have achieved a transformed understanding of what politics can accomplish and what it requires.

This transformation in political understanding extends to how societies conceptualize citizenship and civic participation itself. Deeply divided societies tend toward two problematic extremes: either hyper-politicization, where every aspect of life becomes a battleground in larger conflicts, or withdrawal from public engagement by those exhausted by constant confrontation. Both patterns undermine the kind of citizenship that reunification requires—engaged enough to participate in collective decision-making but not so consumed by political identity that difference becomes intolerable. When understanding transforms, societies sometimes develop what might be called proportional citizenship—ways of being engaged in public life that acknowledge politics' importance without making it totalizing, that create space for domains of life not primarily organized around partisan division, that allow people to hold political commitments seriously while maintaining relationships across political differences, and that recognize that the work of sustaining shared life requires both political engagement and activities that exist somewhat outside the political realm. This balanced citizenship appears when people can participate in political campaigns while also engaging in community service organizations, religious congregations, artistic collaborations, or recreational activities that bring together people with diverse political views around shared interests. It emerges when schools teach civic engagement in ways that emphasize both the importance of political participation and the dangers of reducing all human relationships to political categories. It develops when public spaces and institutions create opportunities for people to encounter one another as neighbors, colleagues, fellow enthusiasts, or fellow sufferers, rather than only as political allies or opponents. When societies protect these domains of shared life while still maintaining vigorous democratic debate, they demonstrate understanding that humans are always more than their political identities and that reunification requires honoring that fullness. The transformation lies in achieving an appropriate balance rather than swinging between the extremes of treating politics as everything or nothing, recognizing instead that citizenship in diverse democracies requires engagement that is simultaneously serious and bounded, passionate but not totalizing.

The dawn of transformed understanding ultimately manifests in changed relationships to the future and to possibility itself. Societies trapped in intense conflict often experience a kind of temporal claustrophobia where the present conflicts seem so all-consuming that imagining genuinely different futures becomes nearly impossible. The categories through which people understand their world—the divisions between us and them, the narratives about who we are and who threatens us—become so reified that they feel like permanent features of reality rather than contingent social constructions that might be transformed. One of the most profound indicators that understanding has genuinely shifted appears when societies recover the ability to imagine futures that are not simply extensions of present conflicts or returns to imagined pasts, but genuinely novel arrangements that honor both continuity with the past and creative adaptation to changing circumstances. This recovered imagination shows itself when communities begin articulating aspirations for their collective life that do not require the defeat or disappearance of those they currently oppose, when they develop visions of flourishing that make space for those with whom they disagree, and when they can identify shared interests and collective goods even while maintaining their particular identities and commitments. The transformation appears not in fantasy that eliminates all conflict, but in an expanded sense of what remains possible despite conflict, in recognition that social arrangements are human creations that can be reimagined and reconstructed rather than iron laws to be endured. When societies that seemed locked in irreconcilable conflict begin producing artistic works, policy proposals, and public conversations that imagine futures of genuine coexistence, when young people in particular can envision lives not defined primarily by the conflicts that shaped their parents' generation, when innovation and experimentation become possible because the future has opened beyond the narrow parameters of present division, understanding has transformed in ways that make reunification not merely conceivable but actively pursuable as a realistic rather than utopian aspiration.

This transformed relationship to possibility particularly matters because it creates conditions for the kind of ongoing adaptation that reunification requires. The processes we have examined throughout earlier explorations—dialogue, trust-building, community healing—never reach completion but require constant renewal in changing circumstances. New conflicts emerge, old grievances resurface in unexpected forms, changing demographics alter the landscape of diversity, and global forces introduce novel challenges that test established arrangements. Societies locked in rigid understandings lack the flexibility to adapt to such changes without experiencing them as threats to fundamental identity. When understanding has transformed, however, societies develop what might be called adaptive resilience—the capacity to maintain commitment to core principles of inclusion, justice, and mutual regard while continuously adjusting the specific forms these commitments take in response to changing circumstances. This adaptive capacity appears when societies can reform institutions that are not serving everyone well without experiencing such reform as a loss of identity, when they can incorporate new groups into their understanding of "us" without feeling that existing groups have been displaced, and when they can respond to emerging challenges with creativity rather than reflexive defensiveness or paralyzed anxiety. South Africa's ongoing efforts to expand its post-apartheid framework of Rainbow Nation identity to incorporate ongoing difficulties of inequality, xenophobia toward other African immigrants, and generational change demonstrate this kind of adaptive work—not successfully resolving all tensions but maintaining a commitment to an inclusive democratic vision while continuously adapting its specific instantiations. When societies develop such adaptive capacity, understanding shifts from rigid attachment to specific arrangements to principled flexibility that can honor core commitments while remaining responsive to changing realities.

The transformation of understanding we have explored throughout this chapter represents neither a final destination nor an automatic outcome of the processes examined in previous explorations. Societies can engage in dialogue, build bridges, cultivate empathy, reconstruct trust, heal communities, and still fall back into division if the more profound transformation of understanding does not occur. Equally, such transformation cannot be directly engineered or mandated but emerges, when it does, from the accumulated effects of countless individual shifts in perspective, institutional reforms, cultural changes, and deliberate choices to approach difference with curiosity rather than defensiveness. What makes this dawn of new understanding both precious and precarious is that it represents a genuinely emergent phenomenon—more than the sum of its parts, yet dependent on those parts for its existence and sustenance. The narrative sophistication, epistemological maturity, tragic wisdom, temporal understanding, civic balance, and expanded imagination we have examined do not arise through any single intervention but through the interaction of multiple processes operating at different scales over extended time periods. They require both intentional cultivation and patient acceptance that transformation follows its own timeline, both an ambitious vision and humble recognition that understanding can regress as well as develop, and both sustained effort and appreciation for the profound difficulty of what reunification attempts. As societies continue the work of healing their divisions, the emergence of transformed understanding provides both inspiration that genuine change remains possible and a sobering reminder that such change requires more than techniques or procedures, demanding instead a fundamental reorientation in how we perceive ourselves, our differences, and our shared fate. When such reorientation begins to dawn in societies that have undertaken the arduous journey through dialogue and toward reunification, possibilities open that were invisible within the narrower understandings that division produced, offering hope not for the elimination of all conflict but for its transformation into something generative rather than destructive, into the creative tension from which genuinely inclusive societies might emerge.

Chapter 11: The Role of Leadership in Unity

The transformation of fractured societies from division to understanding ultimately depends on countless individual acts of courage, empathy, and commitment distributed across entire populations. Yet history persistently demonstrates that these distributed efforts require catalyzation, direction, and protection from forces that would undermine them. Leadership emerges not as a substitute for broad-based participation in reunification, but as an essential amplifying mechanism that shapes the contexts in which millions of smaller choices are made. The question facing divided societies is not whether leadership matters—it clearly does—but rather what forms of leadership advance reunification rather than merely consolidating the power of one faction over others, and how such leadership can be cultivated, recognized, and sustained through the long arc of social healing.

Traditional conceptions of leadership in times of social crisis often default to charismatic individuals who transcend ordinary politics through force of personality, moral authority, or rhetorical brilliance. Nelson Mandela, Mahatma Gandhi, Martin Luther King Jr.—these towering figures dominate our imagination when we think about leadership that transforms conflict. Yet this focus on exceptional individuals, while understandable, obscures more than it reveals about the actual leadership ecosystems required for reunification at scale. The charismatic individual model creates several problems: it makes reunification seem dependent on the random appearance of rare genius; it encourages passive waiting for the right leader rather than active cultivation of leadership capacity throughout society; and it fails to capture the distributed, networked, and often unglamorous leadership work that actually sustains reunification efforts over the decades required for genuine transformation. What societies emerging from deep division actually need is not primarily a single transformational figure but rather what might be called "leadership density"—a sufficient concentration of people at multiple levels and in various sectors who understand the nature of the divisions, possess skills in bridging them, and maintain commitment to reunification even when it conflicts with short-term factional advantage.

This leadership density cannot emerge spontaneously or through wishful thinking. It requires deliberate cultivation through institutions and practices specifically designed to develop capacities that do not arise naturally from our tribal instincts. Political systems designed on winner-take-all principles systematically select against the kinds of leaders most valuable for reunification, instead rewarding those who most effectively mobilize their base through sharpening rather than softening distinctions. Educational systems that segregate students by geography, class, or ideology produce leaders who have never developed the skills of genuinely engaging with different perspectives. Professional tracks in politics, media, activism, and community organization that offer no rewards for bridge-building and no penalties for inflammatory rhetoric create perverse incentive structures that drive talent away from reunification work. The cultivation of leadership density, therefore, requires institutional reforms that change the selection pressures operating on aspiring leaders, creating pathways to influence and authority that favor unifying rather than dividing approaches. Some societies have experimented with electoral systems requiring coalition formation, mandatory power-sharing arrangements in divided regions, and leadership development programs that deliberately bring together emerging leaders from opposing factions before divisions calcify into permanent hostility. These structural approaches recognize that leadership for unity must be systematically cultivated rather than merely hoped for.

Beyond questions of how unifying leaders are developed lies the equally crucial question of what such leaders actually do that proves effective in healing divisions. One essential function involves what might be termed "narrative reframing"—the capacity to tell the story of the conflict in ways that create openings for movement beyond entrenched positions. Every prolonged social division generates narratives that explain the conflict, assign blame, and justify each faction's position. These narratives become remarkably resistant to contrary evidence because they serve essential psychological and social functions for those who hold them, providing meaning, identity, and moral clarity. Leaders who facilitate reunification do not simply deny these narratives or replace them with equally one-sided alternatives favoring different factions. Instead, they develop more complex narratives that acknowledge the legitimate grievances and genuine suffering of multiple parties while creating space for movement beyond the paralysis of competing victimhoods. Abraham Lincoln's second inaugural address provides a canonical example: "Both read the same Bible and pray to the same God, and each invokes His aid against the other... The prayers of both could not be answered. Neither has been answered fully. The Almighty has His own purposes." This narrative reframing acknowledged the moral seriousness with which both sides approached the conflict while locating both within a larger framework that made reconciliation conceivable without requiring either side to accept the other's account of the war's meaning. Modern leaders attempting reunification face similar challenges in developing narratives that honor different experiences of division while opening pathways beyond it.

Another crucial leadership function involves what organizational theorists call "holding the tension"—

maintaining commitment to reunification even when it generates intense discomfort for all parties. Reunification processes necessarily create periods where everyone feels dissatisfied: those who suffered under previous arrangements feel reconciliation happens too quickly and without sufficient acknowledgment of their pain; those invested in the old order feel they are being unfairly blamed and asked to surrender too much; and moderates in the middle feel caught between extremes that seem to grow more rather than less vocal as reunification processes unfold. Leaders who successfully navigate these tensions do not simply split differences or seek lowest-common-denominator compromises that satisfy no one. Instead, they help societies endure the discomfort of genuine transformation, repeatedly articulating why the pain of remaining divided exceeds the discomfort of reunification, and demonstrating through their own conduct that holding this tension is both necessary and survivable. This requires unusual emotional resilience and what psychologists call "distress tolerance"—the capacity to remain functional and strategic even when experiencing significant psychological discomfort. Political leaders who cannot tolerate the anxiety of disappointing various constituencies will either abandon reunification efforts when they become difficult or will pursue superficial compromises that address symptoms rather than causes. The leadership development imperative, therefore, includes helping potential leaders build the capacity to sustain complex processes through inevitable periods of resistance and backlash.

Leaders advancing reunification must also address the paradox of speaking simultaneously to multiple audiences with fundamentally different understandings of the conflict. Every statement directed toward one constituency gets interpreted through the frameworks and concerns of others, creating constant potential for misunderstanding and accusations of betrayal. Another may interpret a leader who acknowledges legitimate grievances of one faction as endorsing extremist positions. Attempts to honor the complexity of situations can be read as moral equivocation or a lack of courage. This communicative challenge requires developing what might be called "multilingual fluency"—not in the linguistic sense but in the capacity to speak in ways that register meaningfully across different worldviews and value systems. Some leaders develop this fluency through personal biography that spans multiple worlds; others acquire it through disciplined study of the concerns, symbols, and reasoning patterns meaningful to different constituencies. The key is developing the capacity to translate concepts across frameworks without either distorting the message beyond recognition or speaking in such vague generalities that the communication becomes meaningless. This translational leadership represents one of the most demanding cognitive and communicative challenges facing those who would help societies reunify, requiring constant navigation between the Scylla of alienating some constituencies through excessive accommodation of others and the Charybdis of satisfying no one through bland platitudes.

 The ethical dimensions of leadership in divided societies deserve particular attention because the very exercise of leadership in such contexts involves moral complexities that differ significantly from leadership in more unified settings. In relatively cohesive societies, leaders can generally assume shared frameworks for evaluating what constitutes legitimate authority and appropriate exercise of power. In deeply divided societies, these frameworks themselves become contested, and leaders must navigate situations where their authority is recognized by some constituencies but actively rejected by others. This creates what political philosophers call "legitimacy pluralism"—the existence of multiple, incompatible standards for evaluating whether leadership exercises are justified. A leader who derives authority from a democratic election may face communities who reject that election as illegitimate; a leader who emerges from moral or religious authority may encounter secularized populations for whom such sources of legitimacy carry no weight; a leader recognized through traditional or customary systems may find this authority challenged by those who see such systems as oppressive. Navigating this pluralism requires particular ethical sophistication: excessive insistence on one's preferred legitimacy framework may further divide rather than unite, while abandoning all claims to legitimate authority renders leadership impossible. Effective leaders in these contexts typically develop what might be called "legitimacy portfolios"—drawing on multiple sources of authority (democratic mandate, moral exemplarity, technical expertise, traditional standing, proven bridge-building success) so that different constituencies can recognize legitimacy through other pathways. This approach acknowledges that reunification cannot wait for agreement on fundamental political philosophy but must proceed through pragmatic accommodation of other ways of understanding authority itself.

The temporal dimensions of leadership for reunification require understanding that healing of deep divisions unfolds across timeframes that exceed individual political careers or even individual lifetimes. This temporal reality creates distinctive leadership challenges because political systems typically operate on much shorter cycles— election terms, budget years, news cycles—that put pressure on leaders to deliver demonstrable short-term results. Leaders who attempt to align their reunification efforts with these short cycles almost inevitably pursue surface-level reconciliation that addresses visible symptoms while leaving root causes untouched. Genuine reunification requires leaders who can think and plan across extended timeframes while still achieving sufficient short-term progress to maintain political viability and popular support. This balancing act necessitates what developmental psychologists call "nested temporality"—the capacity to operate simultaneously on multiple time horizons, pursuing immediate confidence-building measures that demonstrate good faith while laying groundwork for transformations that will only bear fruit years or decades later. Some societies have attempted to institutionalize this temporal complexity through mechanisms like multi-year peace processes with staged implementation, truth and reconciliation commissions whose work unfolds over years, or constitutional conventions that operate outside normal political timeframes. The leadership challenge involves maintaining coherence across these different temporal scales, ensuring that short-term actions remain consistent with long-term visions rather than undermining them through expedient compromises.

The relationship between formal and informal leadership deserves careful examination, as reunification processes depend heavily on leadership operating outside conventional political structures. While heads of state, legislators, and senior officials play crucial roles, much of the actual bridge-building work happens through what political scientists call "Track Two" processes—unofficial dialogues, civil society initiatives, professional networks, and community-level organizing that occurs beneath the radar of formal politics. Leaders in these informal spaces often possess greater freedom to experiment, take risks, and build relationships across dividing lines because they operate with lower visibility and less accountability to rigid constituencies. Yet they typically lack the formal authority and resources to implement changes at scale. Effective reunification ecosystems require productive relationships between these two spheres of leadership, with informal leaders laying the groundwork that formal leaders can later institutionalize, and formal leaders creating a protective space within which informal bridge-building can proceed without being crushed by hardline opposition. The civil rights movement in the United States provides instructive examples: formal political leaders like Presidents Kennedy and Johnson could only move as far as political conditions permitted, while informal leaders like the organizers of the Freedom Rides and sit-ins created political pressure and new social facts that expanded what became politically possible. The relationship was neither smooth nor without tension— informal leaders often viewed formal political leaders as timid or compromised, while political leaders saw movement activists as naive about political realities. Yet the combination of both forms of leadership ultimately achieved transformations that neither could have accomplished alone. Contemporary divided societies need to understand these dynamics and create structures that facilitate rather than obstruct such productive tensions between formal and informal leadership.

The psychology of followership provides essential context for understanding leadership in reunification because the relationship between leaders and constituencies differs fundamentally in divided versus unified societies. In relatively cohesive societies, followers generally share leaders' basic goals, even when they disagree about methods or pace. In divided societies, constituencies often follow leaders not because they share a vision for reunification but because they believe those leaders will protect their interests against those who threaten them. This creates a persistent tension: constituencies often select leaders based on their capacity to win conflict rather than resolve it, but then expect those same leaders to pursue reunification without making concessions that might disadvantage their faction. Leaders attempting to bridge divisions, therefore, constantly face accusations of betrayal from their own base, as any genuine compromise appears as surrender to those who see politics as zero-sum. This dynamic helps explain why leaders who enter peace processes as hardliners sometimes prove more effective than moderates: figures like Menachem Begin and Anwar Sadat, or F.W. de Klerk, had credibility with their own hardline constituencies precisely because they had established reputations as uncompromising defenders of their faction's interests. When such leaders make compromises, they cannot be easily dismissed as weak or naive. This "Nixon goes to China" phenomenon suggests that leadership development for reunification should not focus exclusively on temperamentally moderate individuals but also provide hardline leaders with pathways to bridge-building that do not require them to repudiate their previous commitments or sacrifice credibility with their base.

The institutional positioning of leadership matters enormously for reunification outcomes because leaders need not only personal capacities and intentions but also structural power to protect and advance reunification processes against opposition. History provides numerous examples of well-intentioned leaders with insufficient institutional authority to sustain reunification efforts through periods of backlash and resistance. The location of leadership—whether in executive authority, legislative bodies, judicial systems, military structures, religious institutions, media organizations, or civil society— determines which interventions are possible and which forms of opposition must be overcome. Effective reunification typically requires leadership distributed across multiple institutions rather than concentrated in any single location, as different institutional positions offer different leverage points for advancing reconciliation. Executive leaders can establish commissions, allocate resources, and set public agendas; legislative leaders can craft laws that entrench protections and create incentives; judicial leaders can interpret constitutions in ways that protect minority rights and limit majoritarian domination; military leaders can restrain security forces from actions that inflame tensions; religious leaders can mobilize moral authority and provide sacred framing for reconciliation; media leaders can shape information environments in ways that facilitate rather than obstruct understanding; and civil society leaders can organize grassroots participation in reconciliation processes. The leadership challenge involves not identifying single transformational figures but instead building sufficient leadership capacity across this entire ecosystem so that reunification efforts can proceed even when facing opposition from some institutional quarters.

The cultivation of successor leadership represents perhaps the least appreciated but most crucial function of leadership for reunification. Leaders who successfully advance the healing of social divisions often achieve iconic status, making their personal authority central to reunification processes. This creates a dangerous vulnerability because leadership transitions can trigger renewed conflict if constituencies lose faith that successors will continue protecting their interests. The death of Yugoslavia's Tito, the retirement of Singapore's Lee Kuan Yew, and the transition in South Africa under Mandela—each created moments of uncertainty in which carefully constructed arrangements faced testing. Wise leaders for reunification, therefore, focus not merely on achieving progress during their own tenure but on institutionalizing that progress and developing successor leadership that can sustain momentum. This requires deliberately building what organizational theorists call "leadership pipelines"— systematic processes for identifying, training, and positioning the next generation of leaders who will carry forward reunification work. Some aspects of leadership capacity can be taught through formal programs in negotiation, dialogue facilitation, conflict resolution, and intercultural competence. Other aspects emerge through experience and cannot be transmitted through classroom instruction. The most effective approaches combine both:

creating opportunities for emerging leaders to engage in actual bridge-building work under the mentorship of more experienced practitioners, gradually increasing responsibility as capacities develop. Societies that treat leadership for reunification as a permanent function requiring continuous cultivation prove far more resilient than those dependent on particular individuals, however gifted those individuals might be.

The question of how societies recognize authentic leadership for reunification versus manipulative leadership that merely performs unity while advancing factional interests requires developing what might be called "discernment capacity" across entire populations. Not every leader who speaks the language of reconciliation genuinely pursues it; some master the rhetoric of bridge-building while conducting business-as-usual factional politics or even deepening divisions through subtler means. This capacity for manipulation proves especially dangerous because it inoculates populations against genuine reunification efforts—having been fooled by false promises of unity, people become cynical about any such appeals. Developing societal discernment requires moving beyond naïve faith in leaders' stated intentions to evaluate actual patterns of behavior over time. Leaders genuinely committed to reunification demonstrate several characteristic patterns: they make costly sacrifices of short-term factional advantage for long-term shared benefit; they maintain consistency between what they say to different audiences rather than telling each what it wants to hear; they build diverse coalitions that include people from various factions rather than surrounding themselves only with loyalists; they welcome accountability mechanisms and constraints on their own authority rather than seeking to concentrate power; and they invest in institutional changes that will outlast their own tenure rather than remaining dependent on their personal authority. Educational systems, media organizations, and civil society institutions all play roles in helping citizens develop the capacity to recognize these patterns and distinguish genuine from performative leadership for unity.

The sustainability of leadership for reunification ultimately depends on creating social and political conditions where such leadership becomes not exceptional but normal—where bridge-building and reconciliation represent mainstream rather than fringe approaches to politics and social organization. This normalization requires transforming the incentive structures that currently often punish leaders who pursue reunification while rewarding those who deepen divisions. As long as political systems, media ecosystems, and fundraising mechanisms provide greater rewards for divisive than for unifying leadership, societies will continue to struggle to generate sufficient leadership density for genuine healing. The transformation of these systems represents perhaps the most challenging aspect of reunification because it requires persuading those who currently benefit from division to accept structural changes that would reduce their advantages. Yet history demonstrates that such transformations can occur when the costs of continued division become sufficiently apparent and when enough institutional actors recognize that their own long-term interests lie in reunification rather than continued conflict. The leaders who facilitate such systemic transformation may never receive the recognition accorded to more visible reconciliation figures. Still, they perform equally essential work in creating conditions where reunification can become self-sustaining rather than dependent on exceptional individuals willing to sacrifice everything for healing that may not fully arrive during their lifetimes. The most profound leadership for unity may ultimately consist not in performing spectacular acts of reconciliation but in patiently constructing the institutional architecture within which thousands of smaller acts of bridge-building become possible, valued, and eventually routine.

The intersection of leadership and democratic legitimacy presents particularly acute challenges in societies attempting reunification after periods of authoritarian rule or civil conflict. New democratic institutions require leaders who can simultaneously establish the authority of these institutions while demonstrating flexibility and restraint in exercising the power they confer. This dual mandate creates tensions that less experienced democracies often struggle to navigate: leaders must be strong enough to protect fragile democratic processes from those who would undermine them, yet sufficiently restrained to avoid the authoritarian tendencies that contributed to division in the first place. Eastern European countries transitioning from communism faced these dilemmas acutely—leaders needed authority to dismantle old power structures and establish new institutions. Still, excessive concentration of authority in reformist hands sometimes reproduced the very centralization of power they sought to overcome. Poland's gradual transition, involving negotiated power-sharing between Solidarity and reformed communists, proved more stable than rapid transitions elsewhere precisely because it allowed multiple leadership centers to develop simultaneously, preventing any single faction from claiming a monopoly on legitimate authority. The leadership lesson is that democratic reunification requires not the strongest possible executive authority but rather the cultivation of multiple centers of legitimate power that can check and balance each other while maintaining sufficient coordination to govern effectively.

The role of international leadership and external actors in facilitating domestic reunification warrants examination, as divided societies rarely exist in isolation from broader regional and global contexts. International leaders—whether representing governments, multilateral institutions, or transnational civil society organizations—can provide resources, expertise, and political pressure that domestic actors alone cannot mobilize. The international community's role in Northern Ireland's peace process, the Truth and Reconciliation Commission in South Africa, and post-conflict reconstruction in Rwanda all demonstrate how external leadership can amplify domestic efforts toward reunification. Yet international involvement also risks undermining domestic ownership of reconciliation processes, creating dependencies on external resources and validation that prove unsustainable when international attention inevitably shifts elsewhere. The most effective external leadership operates on principles of subsidiarity— providing support that enhances rather than substitutes for domestic leadership capacity, gradually transferring responsibility as local capabilities develop, and resisting the temptation to impose solutions that reflect international preferences rather than local realities. International leaders must also recognize the limits of their understanding— outsiders rarely grasp the full complexity of regional divisions, the historical depth of grievances, or the cultural contexts within which reconciliation must unfold. The leadership challenge for international actors is to maintain sufficient humility about these limitations while still providing the support that struggling societies desperately need.

The generational dimensions of leadership for reunification reflect the reality that different age cohorts experience divisions differently and require different kinds of leadership to engage them effectively. Older generations who lived through the most acute phases of conflict carry direct memories of violence, betrayal, and loss that shape their receptivity to reconciliation appeals. Younger generations who grew up after the worst conflicts may lack these visceral memories but inherit trauma and grievance through family narratives and cultural socialization. Leadership that resonates with older generations—often emphasizing acknowledgment of past suffering and careful protection of hard-won gains—may seem excessively cautious or backward-looking to younger people eager to move beyond historical grievances their peers on the other side of dividing lines never personally committed. Conversely, youth-oriented leadership emphasizing radical transformation and rapid reconciliation may terrify older people who remember how quickly situations can deteriorate. Effective reunification ecosystems require leadership that spans generations, with older leaders providing wisdom, historical perspective, and credibility born of lived experience. In comparison, younger leaders inject energy, fresh thinking, and a willingness to challenge inherited assumptions that may no longer serve reconciliation purposes. The intergenerational transmission of leadership becomes crucial, creating opportunities for younger leaders to learn from elder statesmen and women. In contrast, elder leaders develop the capacity to listen to and incorporate the perspectives of generations with different experiences and aspirations. Some societies have institutionalized this through formal councils or advisory bodies that deliberately include multiple generations, creating structured dialogue across age cohorts rather than leaving generational relations to chance.

Chapter 12: The Path Forward Together

The reunification of society is not a destination but a continuous journey that demands constant renewal, adaptation, and commitment from each generation. Having explored the foundational concepts of dialogue, empathy, institutional reform, and visionary leadership, we now face the practical question that determines whether all previous insights amount to anything more than sophisticated theory: how do we actually move forward together, translating understanding into sustained action that transforms the lived reality of divided communities? This chapter examines the specific practices, organizational structures, and collective disciplines that convert aspiration into achievement, recognizing that the gap between knowing what should be done and actually accomplishing it often proves wider than the distance between ignorance and knowledge.

The transition from insight to implementation requires what might be called "applied reunification"—the development of concrete methodologies, organizational frameworks, and accountability systems that embed reunification principles into the actual operations of institutions, communities, and daily life. This goes beyond the inspirational calls to unity or the theoretical frameworks for understanding division that we have examined. It demands the creation of what organizational theorists call "operational systems"—the routines, protocols, measurement frameworks, and feedback mechanisms that ensure intentions actually shape behavior and that episodic efforts evolve into sustained practices. In South Africa's post-apartheid transformation, for instance, the inspiring vision of the Rainbow Nation and the profound work of the Truth and Reconciliation Commission had to be supplemented by thousands of specific operational decisions: how schools would integrate students from different backgrounds, what procedures businesses would follow to address employment inequities, how municipal services would be delivered equitably across neighborhoods with vastly different historical access to infrastructure. The vision provided direction, but operational systems determined whether transformation happened in practice or remained aspirational rhetoric. Similarly, in post-conflict Northern Ireland, the Good Friday Agreement established political frameworks. Still, the actual peace was built through countless operational decisions about police reform, educational reform, symbolic representation in public spaces, and resource allocation. The lesson from these and similar experiences is that reunification requires both inspirational vision and mundane operational competence—the ability to translate principles into procedures, values into measurable outcomes, and commitments into organizational routines that persist even when initial enthusiasm wanes.

Creating operational systems for reunification begins with developing what we might call "reunification infrastructure"—the organizational platforms, communication channels, resource allocation mechanisms, and accountability structures specifically designed to support ongoing bridging work across dividing lines. This infrastructure differs fundamentally from traditional institutions in several respects. First, it operates horizontally across existing institutional boundaries rather than vertically within single organizations, recognizing that division typically manifests between rather than within formal structures. A reunification infrastructure might include cross-sector councils that bring together representatives from government, business, civil society, religious communities, and cultural organizations—not for occasional ceremonial meetings but for sustained collaborative work on specific challenges. In Medellín,

Colombia, the city's transformation from one of the world's most violent urban areas to an internationally recognized model of social innovation depended significantly on creating such infrastructure, including innovation districts that deliberately bridged wealthy and poor neighborhoods, public libraries designed as community gathering spaces in marginalized areas, and cable car systems that literally connected hillside slums to downtown economic opportunities. These were not merely construction projects but infrastructure investments explicitly designed to bridge social divisions and create new patterns of interaction across class lines that historical development patterns had separated.

Second, adequate reunification infrastructure operates at multiple scales simultaneously—neighborhood, municipal, regional, and national—with mechanisms for coordination across these levels that allow local innovations to inform broader policy. In contrast, national frameworks create enabling conditions for local experimentation. The absence of such multi-scale coordination explains why many well-intentioned reunification efforts fail to achieve lasting impact. A neighborhood dialogue program might help improve relations among community members. Still, if municipal policies or national political rhetoric continue to reinforce division, the local success remains isolated and fragile. Conversely, national reconciliation initiatives often fail to gain traction because they lack mechanisms for translation into locally relevant practices that address specific community contexts. The Canadian Truth and Reconciliation Commission's work on Indigenous-settler relations illustrates both the necessity and difficulty of multi-scale infrastructure. The national commission created a framework and documented historical abuses. Still, actual reconciliation requires implementation through provincial governments, municipal services, educational institutions, healthcare systems, and countless other organizations, each with different jurisdictions, capacities, and levels of commitment. The commission's 94 Calls to Action provided a coordinating framework, but implementation infrastructure—tracking mechanisms, accountability systems, resource allocation processes, and coordination bodies—has proven as important as the initial recommendations themselves. Without such infrastructure spanning multiple scales, even well-conceived initiatives dissipate their energy due to a lack of coordination and mutual reinforcement.

The creation of reunification infrastructure must address a fundamental paradox: institutions designed to bridge divisions inevitably have their own institutional interests, power dynamics, and tendency toward self-perpetuation that can ultimately subvert their reunification mission. History provides numerous examples of reconciliation commissions, peace-building organizations, and diversity offices that evolved from transformative catalysts into bureaucratic fixtures more concerned with their own survival than with the challenging work they were created to accomplish. Preventing such institutional capture requires building self-limiting and self-evaluating mechanisms into the reunification infrastructure from its inception. This might include sunset provisions that require periodic renewal based on demonstrated progress toward measurable reunification outcomes rather than mere organizational activity, governance structures that give those most affected by division meaningful power over institutional priorities rather than merely consulting them, and transparent measurement systems that track outcomes rather than simply counting inputs or activities. The contrast between effective and ineffective reunification infrastructure often lies precisely in these accountability mechanisms. Organizations that primarily track their own activities— number of dialogue sessions held, participants engaged, resources distributed—frequently drift toward self-justification rather than actual impact. Those that rigorously measure changes in actual division indicators—residential integration patterns, cross-group friendship formation, employment equity, political representation, intergroup trust levels—maintain a more explicit focus on their fundamental purpose and can adapt strategies based on what measurably works rather than what feels satisfying to organizational stakeholders.

Beyond organizational infrastructure, the path forward together requires developing what might be termed "reunification literacy"—a set of widely distributed capabilities that enable ordinary citizens to recognize division dynamics, navigate cross-difference interactions constructively, and contribute to bridging efforts in their own spheres of influence. Just as civic literacy programs teach citizens to understand governmental structures and democratic processes, reunification literacy programs would teach recognition of in-group/out-group dynamics, the formation and interruption of stereotypes, constructive conflict engagement, perspective-taking across difference, and practical skills for building relationships across dividing lines. This is not merely about elite reconciliation practitioners developing sophisticated techniques but about democratizing reunification capabilities so they become part of ordinary civic competence. Finland's extensive education in media literacy and critical thinking, for instance, has helped create population-level resilience against disinformation and manipulation that exploits social divisions. By teaching all students to recognize propaganda techniques, verify information sources, and understand how emotional manipulation works, Finnish education has distributed defensive capabilities against division throughout the population rather than depending solely on expert fact-checkers or platform moderators. Similar approaches to reunification literacy would teach citizens to recognize when their emotions are being manipulated to increase out-group hostility, to question narratives that paint entire groups as uniformly threatening, and to practice specific communication techniques that de-escalate rather than inflame cross-group tensions.

The development of reunification literacy raises essential questions about where and how such education should occur. Schools represent obvious sites for systematic skill development. Yet, education systems in divided societies are often themselves contested terrain where conflicts over curriculum, language, historical narrative, and cultural representation regularly intensify rather than bridge divisions. The Northern Ireland education system, for instance, remains substantially segregated along Protestant-Catholic lines decades after the Good Friday Agreement, with most children attending schools that primarily serve their own community. Integrated schools exist but remain a small minority, and debates over their expansion immediately become entangled with broader questions about identity, culture, and community autonomy. This suggests that while school-based education remains essential, reunification literacy cannot depend solely on formal education systems. Alternative approaches include workplace training programs that help organizations navigate diversity constructively, community center programs that reach adults outside formal education, media literacy campaigns that use public platforms to build critical thinking capabilities, and cultural programming that models constructive cross-difference engagement through storytelling, performance, and participatory arts. The Broadcasting Corporation in post-genocide Rwanda, for instance, created radio programming that deliberately modeled constructive intergroup dialogue and problem-solving, using serialized dramas to teach conflict resolution skills and perspective-taking while entertaining audiences. Such approaches recognize that reunification literacy must be developed across entire populations through multiple channels rather than assuming formal education alone can provide necessary capabilities.

The path forward together also requires confronting difficult questions about pace, sequencing, and the relationship between immediate needs and long-term transformation. Societies in acute crisis often face urgent pressures for visible action that can conflict with the patient, relationship-building work that deeper reunification requires. When violence is ongoing, inequality is extreme, or political dysfunction is paralytic, calls for incremental dialogue processes can seem inadequate to the urgency of the moment. Yet rushed reconciliation efforts that prioritize speed over depth often yield superficial agreements that collapse under pressure or performative gestures that foster cynicism rather than genuine bridging. Managing this tension between urgency and sustainability requires a sophisticated understanding of what organizational change theorists call "pace layering"—the recognition that different dimensions of transformation operate on different timescales and effective change requires coordinating across these temporal layers. Some actions—stopping active violence, providing emergency relief, implementing basic security measures—must happen immediately and cannot wait for slow trust-building. Other dimensions—addressing root causes of conflict, transforming institutional cultures, rebuilding trust across communities—necessarily require sustained effort over years or decades. Still other aspects— generational healing, cultural transformation, the full integration of traumatic history into collective memory— operate on timescales of decades or generations. Effective reunification strategies sequence interventions appropriately, using short-term actions not as substitutes for longer-term work but as foundations that enable more profound transformation. The peace process in Mozambique illustrates this principle through its combination of immediate military demobilization, medium-term political integration, and long-term community reconciliation efforts. While all three dimensions were necessary, attempting to accomplish everything simultaneously would have overwhelmed limited implementation capacity, whereas sequencing allowed earlier achievements to create conditions for subsequent stages.

Central to navigating an appropriate pace and sequencing is developing realistic expectations about what reunification actually entails and the timeframes required for different outcomes. One of the most damaging patterns in reunification work is the cycle of inflated expectations followed by disappointed disillusionment when rapid transformation fails to materialize. When reunification is portrayed as achievable through a single symbolic gesture, a single major initiative, or the election of a particular leader, inevitable disappointment follows when deep divisions persist despite these interventions. This disappointment then fuels cynicism, undermining sustained commitment to longer-term work. Breaking this pattern requires honest communication about reunification as generational work requiring sustained effort across multiple dimensions simultaneously. The post-World War II reconciliation between France and Germany provides an instructive perspective on realistic timescales. While political reconciliation occurred relatively quickly through institutions such as the European Coal and Steel Community, cultural reconciliation required decades of school exchanges, city partnerships, and joint historical inquiry. Genuine friendship and integration—the sense that French and Germans were not merely strategic partners but connected peoples with a shared destiny—took a whole generation to develop and required continuous reinforcement through institutional arrangements, cultural exchanges, and political leadership that emphasized partnership. Even 75 years later, the relationship requires ongoing maintenance and remains vulnerable to resurgent nationalism, suggesting that reunification is never definitively complete but must be continuously renewed. Understanding and communicating these realistic timescales helps societies maintain commitment through inevitable difficulties and setbacks rather than abandoning efforts when immediate transformation fails to materialize.

The path forward together must also address questions of resource allocation and the economic dimensions of reunification that are often overshadowed by attention to psychological, cultural, and political factors. While empathy, dialogue, and institutional reform are essential, they remain insufficient if economic conditions continue generating material conflicts that overwhelm bridging efforts. Reunification in deeply unequal societies requires addressing distributional questions directly: how will economic opportunities, public resources, and the benefits of development be shared across communities that division has differentially impacted? These are not merely technical economic questions but fundamentally political ones that test whether reunification rhetoric translates into material reality for those whose lives are most constrained by economic marginalization. The challenge is particularly acute when historical division has created significant economic disparities between groups, such that equitable resource distribution requires not neutral allocation based on current circumstances but deliberate redirection to address historical imbalances. In such contexts, reunification efforts must include economic redistribution components that benefit disadvantaged groups materially, not merely symbolically. South Africa's Black Economic Empowerment policies, despite significant implementation challenges and criticisms, represented recognition that political reconciliation required economic transformation—that asking those who had been systematically excluded from economic opportunity to reconcile without addressing material conditions would undermine the entire reunification project. Similarly, Malaysia's affirmative action policies for Bumiputera populations, however limited, reflected an understanding that maintaining interethnic peace required addressing economic grievances substantively. The lesson is not that any particular redistribution approach is universally applicable, but that reunification strategies must include credible mechanisms to address material grievances and ensure that disadvantaged groups experience tangible improvements in their life circumstances, not merely symbolic recognition.

Economic dimensions of reunification extend beyond redistribution to include deliberate strategies for creating economic interdependence across dividing lines—making different communities materially invested in one another's prosperity rather than viewing each other as economic competitors. This might include integrated supply chains that span communities. These business partnerships require cooperation across groups, regional development strategies that benefit multiple communities simultaneously, and investment in shared infrastructure that creates a common benefit. The European Union's structural funds, which invest in development projects across member states, create such material interdependence—wealthier regions have an interest in the development of poorer ones because integrated markets increase everyone's opportunities. In contrast, recipient regions develop stakes in the continuation of the broader European project. Similar principles can operate at more minor scales. In Bosnia-Herzegovina, specific internationally supported development projects deliberately required cooperation between ethnic communities for implementation, creating practical reasons for engagement beyond merely political reconciliation imperatives. When a water system, electrical grid, or transportation network can only function effectively through cross-community cooperation, practical necessity creates ongoing incentives to maintain working relationships even when political tensions rise. Economic interdependence cannot substitute for trust or replace the need for addressing historical grievances. Still, it lays the material foundations that make backsliding into conflict more costly and cooperation more clearly beneficial.

Technology and digital infrastructure present both opportunities and challenges for the path forward that previous generations of reunification workers did not face. Digital communication technologies enable connection across physical distance, documentation of experiences that might otherwise go unrecorded, and coordination of collective action at scales previously impossible. Yet these same technologies amplify division through algorithmic sorting into ideological bubbles, accelerate misinformation, and create online environments where dehumanizing rhetoric faces fewer social constraints than in face-to-face interaction. The path forward must therefore include digital strategies specifically designed to harness technology's bridging potential while mitigating its dividing effects. This might consist of deliberately designed digital platforms for cross-difference dialogue that use interface design to encourage constructive interaction rather than inflammatory rhetoric, algorithmic curation that intentionally exposes users to diverse perspectives rather than reinforcing existing views, digital literacy education that helps users recognize manipulation and misinformation, and online community standards that maintain space for disagreement while constraining dehumanization. Norway's "The People's Parliament" digital platform, which enables citizens to deliberate on policy questions with exposure to diverse viewpoints and evidence-based information, illustrates how intentional design can create online environments that bridge rather than divide. The platform uses moderation, structured dialogue protocols, and presentation of multiple perspectives to encourage constructive engagement rather than merely amplifying the loudest or most extreme voices.

Such approaches suggest that technology itself is neither inherently divisive nor inherently bridging but can be deliberately shaped to serve reunification purposes when design choices prioritize connection across difference rather than merely maximizing engagement through provocation.

Implementing the path forward together requires attention to motivation—not merely to what should be done, but to why diverse actors with different interests and perspectives would actually commit to doing it. Reunification often faces a mobilization asymmetry: those who profit from division—politically, economically, or psychologically—typically have more substantial incentives to maintain dividing lines than most people have to bridge them. Division provides scapegoats for problems, simplifies complex situations into clear us-versus-them narratives, consolidates in-group solidarity through shared opposition to out-groups, and concentrates benefits among those who position themselves as defenders of their group against external threats. Reunification, in contrast, requires accepting complexity, acknowledging shared responsibility for problems, extending empathy toward those perceived as different, and sharing benefits more broadly. For many people, maintaining division is the path of least resistance, while reunification requires sustained effort against significant obstacles. Overcoming this mobilization asymmetry requires making the benefits of reunification more tangible and immediate than they often appear, while making the costs of continued division more visible than they typically are. This means connecting reunification explicitly to concerns people already have—economic opportunity, community safety, quality of services, children's futures—rather than presenting it as a separate moral imperative disconnected from practical concerns. When reunification can be demonstrated to reduce crime through community cooperation in policing, increase economic opportunity through integrated markets, improve educational outcomes through diverse learning environments, and enhance community resilience through bridging social capital, practical motivations supplement moral ones. Evidence from contact theory research demonstrates that self-interest can indeed align with reunification when conditions are structured appropriately—when intergroup cooperation demonstrably produces better outcomes for everyone than isolation or competition does.

The path forward must also build the capacity to address inevitable setbacks, backsliding, and the resurgence of division even after apparent progress. Reunification is not a linear process but one characterized by advances and retreats, periods of rapid progress and times of stagnation or regression. Societies that have made significant progress toward bridging divisions remain vulnerable to shocks—economic crises, terrorist attacks, external threats, political upheaval—that can rapidly resurrect dormant divisions or create new ones. Resilience in the face of such setbacks requires what disaster preparedness specialists call "anticipatory planning"—identifying potential shock scenarios in advance, developing response protocols that prevent automatic return to division patterns, creating early warning systems that detect emerging tensions before they escalate, and building redundancy into bridging relationships so that damage to some connections does not sever all ties. Rwanda's approach to managing Genocide Memorial Day annually illustrates this principle—the government and civil society organizations have developed extensive protocols for managing this emotionally charged period, including increased community dialogue sessions, mental health support, careful media coverage, and security measures that prevent incidents from escalating. These protocols acknowledge that memorial periods predictably increase tension and prepare responses rather than being surprised when challenges emerge. Similar anticipatory approaches could address other predictable stressors. Electoral campaigns, for instance, regularly inflame divisions in fragmented societies. Yet, few places develop specific reunification protocols for campaign periods—standards for political discourse, bridging events that bring candidates together constructively, media coverage guidelines that avoid inflammatory framing, or post-election reconciliation rituals that help losing sides accept results. Developing such protocols in advance, when tensions are lower, creates resources that can be deployed during predictable stress periods.

Finally, the path forward together requires cultivating what might be called "reunification solidarity"—a form of collective commitment that connects people engaged in this challenging work across different contexts, providing mutual support, shared learning, and encouragement during inevitable difficult periods. Reunification work is emotionally draining, often discouraging, and can be isolating for those who undertake it, particularly when surrounded by cynicism or active opposition. Creating networks that connect peace-builders, dialogue facilitators, bridging leaders, and ordinary citizens committed to reunification across communities and even across countries provides crucial support. International organizations like the International Coalition of Sites of Conscience, which connects museums and heritage sites engaged in memory and reconciliation work, or the Alliance for Peacebuilding, which networks practitioners across conflict zones, illustrate this principle at organizational scales. Similar networks can operate locally, connecting community organizers working on reunification across neighborhoods, or virtually via digital platforms to create peer-support communities. These solidarity networks serve multiple functions: they provide emotional support during difficult periods, enable the sharing of practical strategies and lessons learned, develop accountability systems that maintain commitments to reunification work through peer expectations, and help individual efforts connect to broader movements that provide a sense of collective impact. The civil rights movement's mass meeting tradition, in which activists gathered regularly for mutual encouragement, strategic coordination, and spiritual renewal, demonstrated the sustaining power of reunification solidarity during a long struggle against deeply entrenched division. Contemporary reunification work equally requires such sustaining communities that help committed individuals maintain effort through difficult periods and connect local efforts to broader transformation movements.

The path forward together ultimately depends less on finding perfect strategies or ideal conditions than on developing collective capacity for sustained commitment despite imperfect circumstances, incomplete understanding, and inevitable setbacks. The societies that successfully navigate from deep division toward greater unity do not do so because they found easy paths or possessed unique advantages, but because enough people maintained a commitment to the work across multiple generations, adapting their approaches as circumstances changed while remaining focused on the fundamental project of rebuilding the fractured social fabric. This requires developing what we might call "mature hope"—not the naive optimism that change comes easily or that good intentions alone suffice, but the grounded conviction that sustained collective effort across time can shift seemingly immovable realities. Such hope acknowledges difficulty honestly while refusing to accept division as an inevitable destiny; recognizes that progress happens through the accumulation of small advances rather than sudden transformation; and maintains commitment to the work not because success is guaranteed, but because the alternative—accepting permanent fragmentation—is unacceptable. The path forward is long, complex, and uncertain, but it is a path that can be walked, step by step, choice by choice, by societies that decide their divisions need not define their future.

Bibliography

Appiah, Kwame Anthony. *The Lies That Bind: Rethinking Identity.* New York: Liveright Publishing, 2018.

Assmann, Jan. *Cultural Memory and Early Civilization: Writing, Remembrance, and Political Imagination.* Cambridge: Cambridge University Press, 2011.

Autor, David H., David Dorn, and Gordon H. Hanson. "The China Syndrome: Local Labor Market Effects of Import Competition in the United States." *American Economic Review* 103, no. 6 (2013): 2121–68.

Bail, Christopher A. *Breaking the Social Media Prism: How to Make Our Platforms Less Polarizing.* Princeton, NJ: Princeton University Press, 2021.

Bohm, David. *On Dialogue.* London: Routledge, 1996.

Cacioppo, John T., and William Patrick. *Loneliness: Human Nature and the Need for Social Connection.* New York: W. W. Norton & Company, 2008.

Case, Anne, and Angus Deaton. *Deaths of Despair and the Future of Capitalism.* Princeton, NJ: Princeton University Press, 2020.

Finkel, Eli J., et al. "Political Sectarianism in America." *Science* 370, no. 6516 (2020): 533–36.

Fukuyama, Francis. *Political Order and Political Decay: From the Industrial Revolution to the Globalization of Democracy.* New York: Farrar, Straus and Giroux, 2014.

Gutmann, Amy, and Dennis Thompson. *Why Deliberative Democracy?* Princeton, NJ: Princeton University Press, 2004.

Habermas, Jürgen. *The Structural Transformation of the Public Sphere: An Inquiry into a Category of Bourgeois Society.* Translated by Thomas Burger and Frederick Lawrence. Cambridge, MA: MIT Press, 1991.

Haidt, Jonathan. *The Righteous Mind: Why Good People Are Divided by Politics and Religion.* New York: Vintage Books, 2012.

Hirsch, Marianne. "The Generation of Postmemory." *Poetics Today* 29, no. 1 (2008): 103–28.

Iyengar, Shanto, Guarav Sood, and Yphtach Lelkes. "Affect, Not Ideology: A Social Identity Perspective on Polarization." *Public Opinion Quarterly* 76, no. 3 (2012): 405–31.

Lederach, John Paul. *The Moral Imagination: The Art and Soul of Building Peace.* Oxford: Oxford University Press, 2005.

Levitsky, Steven, and Daniel Ziblatt. *How Democracies Die.* New York: Crown Publishing, 2018.

Mason, Lilliana. *Uncivil Agreement: How Politics Became Our Identity.* Chicago: University of Chicago Press, 2018.

McChesney, Robert W., and John Nichols. *The Death and Life of American Journalism.* New York: Nation Books, 2010.

McPherson, Miller, Lynn Smith-Lovin, and James M. Cook. "Birds of a Feather: Homophily in Social Networks." *Annual Review of Sociology* 27 (2001): 415–44.

Norris, Pippa. *Democratic Deficit: Critical Citizens Revisited.* Cambridge: Cambridge University Press, 2011.

Nussbaum, Martha C. *Creating Capabilities: The Human Development Approach.* Cambridge, MA: Harvard University Press, 2011.

Pariser, Eli. *The Filter Bubble: What the Internet Is Hiding from You.* New York: Penguin Press, 2011.

Pew Research Center. *Political Polarization in the American Public.* Washington, DC: Pew Research Center, 2014. https://www.pewresearch.org/.

Piketty, Thomas. *Capital in the Twenty-First Century.* Translated by Arthur Goldhammer. Cambridge, MA: Harvard University Press, 2014.

Putnam, Robert D. *Bowling Alone: The Collapse and Revival of American Community.* New York: Simon & Schuster, 2000.

Skocpol, Theda. *Diminished Democracy: From Membership to Management in American Civic Life.* Norman: University of Oklahoma Press, 2003.

Sunstein, Cass R. *Going to Extremes: How Like Minds Unite and Divide.* Oxford: Oxford University Press, 2009.

Taylor, Charles. *Modern Social Imaginaries.* Durham, NC: Duke University Press, 2004.

Tocqueville, Alexis de. *Democracy in America*. Translated by Harvey C. Mansfield and Delba Winthrop. Chicago: University of Chicago Press, 2000.

Tufekci, Zeynep. "Algorithmic Harms Beyond Facebook and Google: Emergent Challenges of Computational Agency." *Colorado Technology Law Journal* 13 (2015): 203–18.

Twenge, Jean M. *iGen: Why Today's Super-Connected Kids Are Growing Up Less Rebellious, More Tolerant, Less Happy—and Completely Unprepared for Adulthood.* New York: Atria Books, 2017.

Weber, Max. *The Protestant Ethic and the Spirit of Capitalism.* Translated by Talcott Parsons. London: Routledge, 2005. Initially published in 1905.

Zerubavel, Yael. *Recovered Roots: Collective Memory and the Making of Israeli National Tradition.* Chicago: University of Chicago Press, 1995.

About The Author

Jordan L. Monroe is an acclaimed author, social researcher, and practitioner in community healing and reconciliation. With a background in sociology and public policy, Monroe brings over two decades of experience working with diverse communities striving for unity amid conflict. Her academic contributions, including multiple publications on social change and civic engagement, underscore her expertise in navigating complex societal divisions.

Monroe's passion for fostering dialogue and understanding began as a young activist, and since then, she has been involved in numerous grassroots initiatives aimed at rebuilding trust and cooperation in fractured communities. She has contributed to international conferences and workshops focused on empathy-driven leadership and collective action, providing practical frameworks for engaging communities in meaningful conversations about their shared futures.

In addition to her work as an author, Monroe holds a faculty position at a leading university, where she teaches courses on social movements and conflict resolution. She is a sought-after speaker known for distilling complex sociopolitical issues into actionable insights that inspire hope and collaboration. Through her work, she champions the belief that, despite inherent differences, societies can create pathways for healing and understanding, forging connections that bridge divides and enhance collective well-being.

About The Publisher

Welcome to The Book On Publishing

At The Book On Publishing, we believe in rewriting the rules of learning. Whether you're chasing your next big idea, building a better life, or simply curious about what should have been taught in school, you've come to the right place.

We're a platform built for dreamers, doers, and lifelong learners, offering bold, practical books and tools that empower you to take charge of your journey. From real-world skills to mindset mastery, we publish the book on what matters.

No fluff. No lectures. Just what you need to know, delivered with clarity, purpose, and a spark of curiosity.

Start exploring. Start growing. Start writing your story.

Read more at https://thebookon.ca.

Acknowledgment of AI Assistance

Portions of this book were developed with the support of AI. While every word has been carefully reviewed and refined by the author, AI served as a valuable tool for brainstorming, editing, and structuring ideas. Its assistance helped accelerate the creative process and clarify complex topics.

www.ingramcontent.com/pod-product-compliance
Lightning Source LLC
Chambersburg PA
CBHW060224030426
42335CB00014B/1336